the most they ever had

by rick bragg

the most they ever had

by rick bragg

MACADAM CAGE

MacAdam/Cage
155 Sansome Street, Suite 550
San Francisco, California 94104

www.MacAdamCage.com

Library of Congress Cataloging-in-Publication Data

Bragg, Rick.
The most they ever had / Rick Bragg.
p. cm.
ISBN 978-1-59692-361-4
1. Textile workers—Alabama—Jacksonville—Economic conditions—20th
century. 2. Textile workers—Alabama—Jacksonville—Social conditions--
20th century. 3. Textile workers—Alabama—Jacksonville—Biography. 4.
Jacksonville (Ala.)—Economic conditions—20th century. 5. Jacksonville
(Ala.)—Social conditions—20th century. I. Title.
HD8039.T42U6416 2009
331.7'66700976163—dc22
2009028700

Printed in the United States of America
10 9 8 7 6 5 4 3 2 1

Cover photograph from the collection of Homer Barnwell

Book and jacket design by Dorothy Carico Smith

For the people of the mills

This is what I cannot remember—
a young woman stooped in a field,
the hoe callousing her hands,
the rows stretching out like hours.
And this woman, my mother, rising
to dust rising half a mile
up the road, the car
she has waited days for
realized in the trembling heat.

It will rust until spring, the hoe
dropped at the field's edge.
She is running toward the car,
the sandlapper relatives who spill out
coughing mountain air with lint-filled lungs,
running toward the half-filled grip
she will learn to call a suitcase.

She is dreaming another life,
young enough to believe
it can only be better—
indoor plumbing, eight hour shifts, a man
who waits unknowing for her, a man
who cannot hear through the weave room's
roar the world's soft click,
fate's tumblers falling into place,
soft as the sound of my mother's
bare feet as she runs,
runs toward him, toward me.

—RON RASH

brother

As a boy, I was a little afraid of the people of the mills, of the plain, Pentecostal women in long dresses and waist-length hair, and bony, red-skinned men who still remembered the cut of a cotton sack. They had the look of a people who had not lived life so much as endured it, as if they had walked out of a fire. I would learn not to flinch when some old man offered me a three-fingered hand, or stare at people who seemed to cough all the time, even in fine weather. I knew about work then, in the 1960s and '70s. I swung a pick, ran a chainsaw, toted concrete blocks. But this grit, this sacrifice, was something else. I understood it, finally, one March night in 2001, when I saw a man I believed to be unbreakable just taken apart, not by the mill he served, but something worse.

———

In our boyhood, my big brother, Sam, dug pieces of coal and scrap lumber from the red mud so my mother could heat a borrowed house. In the 1970s, he quit school to load boxcars with one hundred-pound sacks of clay and lime. He shoveled gravel and sand into the backs of flatbed trucks, cut pulpwood, and broke down truck tires with a chisel and a five-pound sledge. Then, he gave me a running start away from all of it.

A hundred times, it seemed, I slouched at the shoulder of some trash-strewn highway in northeastern Alabama, the hood up on a wore-out car, waiting for him to come and get me going again. I was always on my way to some writing job, some frivolous work, something you could do all day and not even get any grease under your nails.

He would pull up in his old Chevrolet pickup, hand me a flashlight—it always seemed I broke down in the dark—and go to work. He would pull wrenches and yank on alternators and water pumps till he peeled the skin off his knuckles, blood mixing with grime until I flipped my clip-on tie over one shoulder and reached in with my free hand, to help. "Quit," he would hiss. "You'll get dirty."

I thought he was the toughest man I ever knew, but now I know he was just as tough as he had to be. He broke bones and let them mend on their own, not to show off, but because insurance was something you got only at a good job. I guess that life broke everything but his heart.

He worked at the end of a shovel handle for twenty years, till he finally landed work at the mill in Jacksonville, Alabama, when he was in his thirties. He armored his body like a medieval knight and went to work in the opening room, where he used bolt cutters to snip steel bands off five hundred-pound bales of cotton. The bales, bound under thousands of pounds of pressure, would explode apart, and the bands, sharp as razor blades, would go winging through the air. I got a call one afternoon to tell me one of the bands had stabbed him in the face under his goggles. A sixteenth of an inch to the right and he would have lost his eye. He was back at work that day.

"Things like that happen," he told me, and shrugged.

I asked him why he risked it.

He ticked the reasons off on his fingers.

Insurance.

Retirement.

Decent money.

A little bit later he got a few pennies more an hour to go work in the mill itself, between rows of spinning steel in a choking cotton dust haze, where every breath drew the potential for disease into his lungs. He was still there in winter of 2001 as rumors thickened that the mill was closing down.

I will never forget how he looked as I walked into my mother's house that night in March, big hands on his knees, afraid. And then I knew. It was a matter of distance, the distance between a hard, hot, dirty, dangerous job, and a shovel handle.

"I don't know…" he began, and then his voice just left him.

He rubbed his face. You could see the permanent stain of grease on his hand, under his skin.

"…what to do."

He had wrecked old trucks into trees when the front ends fell out or the bald tires blew, had jacks slip and cars fall on him, and had tumbled from trees with a chainsaw bucking in his hands. For fun, he walked the mountains in pitch black, chasing his coon dogs across foot-logs and drop-offs where a misstep would leave him freezing in the pines. But what finally scared him, that night, was talk of the end of the world.

———

I decided to write these stories that night, not about him, but people like him, the people of the mill. It has been known by various names—Ide Mill, Profile, Union Yarn—but the people were the same. Each chapter tells a story of a separate life, though the sufferings they endured do run together across the pages. They are grim in many places and sad in spaces in between, but when I told that to a friend, worried that no one would stick with such a book cover to cover, he told me not to worry. "Well, it ain't a damn barn dance, is it? It's an American tragedy."

I know some smart people will say these workers should have known better than to tie their lives so long to such a thing. The world economy changes. Jobs come and go. Business is not in business to make jobs, but money. I understand that, too.

But it seems to me that life made a lot more sense in this country when we made things, built things. "It's got to the point," my brother Sam said, "that the only thing we make in this country is money."

They do not deserve, people this tough, to vanish, not in the clay, and not outside the padlocked doors of their dying industry. But they seem to have few champions. The unions were crushed here, long ago. Their politicians in Washington, forgetting their own history, have pushed for legislation that ignores them, and coddles the rich.

So, as silly as it seems, you write a song for them, a poem, a fable.

This book lends flesh, blood, and bone, I hope, to bloodless numbers in plant closings and layoffs, and in hospital wards and nursing homes and unemployment lines across this land. I hope it honors them, a people once valued for what they could make, how fine it was, and how fast they could make it.

Now the thing they were needed for is going away, or already gone.

They are still here.

the choice

Sometimes the world is flat. In the early spring of 2001, a community of people in the foothills of the Appalachians had come to a falling-off place, to the edge of all they had ever known. Now they stood looking down, angry and afraid. Across the industrial South, padlocks and logging chains bound the doors of silent textile mills, and it seemed a miracle to the blue-collar people in Jacksonville, Alabama, that their cotton mill still bit, shook, and roared. The century-old hardwood floors still trembled under rows of machines, and the people worked on in that mist of white air. The mill had become almost a living thing here, rewarding the hard working and careful with a means of survival, but punishing the careless and clumsy, taking a finger, a hand, more. It was here before the automobile, before the flying machine, and its giant, coal-fired generators lit up the evening sky with the first electricity they ever saw. It roared across generations, and they served it even as it filled their lungs with lint and shortened their lives. In return, the mill let them live in stiff-necked dignity, right here, in the hills of their fathers. So, when death did come, to the red-dirt driveways, mobile homes, and little mill village houses, no one had to ship their bodies home on a train.

———

That spring, Sonny Parker and his wife, Theresa, walked out into the parking lot of the Food Outlet, grocery bags in their hands. The city had three grocery stores, but the Food Outlet is where most of the mill workers brought their paychecks, its aisles crammed with Little Debbie snack cakes, Vienna sausage, and potted meat; its worn tile floors crisscrossed with wobbly buggies pushed by old men in overalls and middle-aged women who had, just minutes before coming inside, carefully combed the last wisps of lint from their hair.

It was just before sunset when Sonny, in his early fifties then, spotted a black leather purse in a grocery buggy. The purse was wide open and seemed to be filled with money.

They stood and stared.

It was money they desperately needed with hard times so close upon them, with Theresa, in her late forties then, so sick from brown lung she could no longer work.

"We didn't touch a dollar," Sonny said.

Sonny picked up the purse and walked back inside the store. He handed it to a manager, who searched inside it for find some kind of identification. "Good Lord, at the money," the manager said. "There's thousands of dollars in this purse."

Sonny was already walking out the door.

The manager found the I.D. and called the woman

who owned it. Sonny and Theresa never heard from her, never even got a thank you.

Sonny shakes his head when he is asked if he was tempted to take it.

"I could have thrown that purse in the truck and driven off, and nobody would have seen me," said Sonny, whose mother worked herself to death in the choking cotton fog of a mill. "I could have took that money and run. But what good would it have done me?

"I didn't earn it."

It is hard to explain to an outsider how money can still be green, can still read twenty dollars, even one hundred dollars, and not be worth anything, not worth a candy wrapper blowing across the parking lot.

It was more than morality, more than Sunday school teaching.

It was his culture.

He went to work in a cotton mill when he was sixteen because he wanted to buy a car, "and no one else was going to buy me one." He and Theresa paid off a little wood-frame house working at the mill, and raised a son and a daughter. "It might not seem like a lot, to some people, what we've got," said Sonny. But they didn't want much, just a decent home, a good-running pickup, and a like-new car every few years. Theresa's brown lung was always seen as a part of the deal, a bargain blue-collar men and women make in their hearts every day.

What can they stand?

What is it worth?

"I wake up in the middle of the night, choking. I sleep in my recliner some nights, to breathe. But I'm not on oxygen yet. I know it's coming, but I am not on it yet," said Theresa, who used to sing the high, sweet notes in a gospel group before the disease took her breath. "I only have to go to the doctor once a month, and there are good days. But me and Sonny, we fed and clothed our family, put our children through school, got them raised. They never wanted for a thing. I was down to ninety-two pounds, at one point, and my daughter would look at me and cry and beg me not to go back. But I had to. I had to choose."

———

Outsiders like to talk about the working people of the Deep South in clichés, like to say their lives are consumed by football, stock car racing, stump jumping, and a whole lot of violent history. But it is work that defines them. You hear it under every shade tree, at every dinner on the ground, whole conversations about timber cut, post holes dug, transmissions pulled.

They do not ask for help from outsiders, unless it is from a preacher, a lawyer, a doctor, people who have skills they do not possess. They can, most of them, lay block, pour concrete, swing a hammer, run a chainsaw, fix a busted water line, and jerk the engine from an American-made car with muscle, a tree limb, and a chain. If their car breaks down at the side of the highway they do not call AAA. They drive the roads with a hydraulic jack, a four-way lug wrench, and a big red tool box that takes two hands to lift and jangles with one thousand leftover screws. They have installed a million radiator hoses by the glow of a Bic lighter, and would have no more left the house without jumper cables than without pants. They know how a septic tank works, how to wire a laundry room, how to safely pull a tick off a two-year-old, and how to unravel a bird's nest from a Daiwa reel.

The women are tougher, still. They know how to compress time, how to work a twelve-hour shift, cook a good supper, run a sewing machine, sing to the baby, ghost-write homework, go to choir practice and the Food Outlet, pick an armload of tomatoes from their own vines, and watch *General Hospital*, at 9 p.m., on the VCR. They eat supper as early as 5 p.m. and are in bed by 10 p.m.—because at 4 a.m. they have to wake up and do it all over again.

They live in little frame houses perched almost on the lip of the highways, in modest brick ranchers on the west side of town, or in the mill village itself, in what used to be company houses. On weekends they drive to Leesburg to fish for crappie, and on Christmas they shoot mistletoe from the high branches of trees. The men—and some of the women—will go at you with a tire iron if you insult them, but they can swallow a lot of bile, if it means a job. They cash their checks, usually, instead of depositing them, because they have to sacrifice the future for the right now. They

play Rook on Saturday nights, and consider fried bologna and canned biscuits to be a first-rate breakfast
food. They know a deer roast tastes less gamey if you
soak it overnight in a pan of buttermilk, and can re-
upholster a pickup seat with a sheet of vinyl, a quarter-
mile of nylon cord, and a pair of needle-nose pliers.

It is the work that makes them, holds them up.
They like the fact they can measure it, see yarn filling
up spools, see how perfect it is. They would hate, most
of them, sitting at an office keyboard, moving phantom money around on a computer screen, then glad-
handing a boss with a real Rolex and a phony smile.
On the mill floor, you never stopped to glad-hand—
the machines would stall, and the chains of production would break.

People who do not work, but could, are despised.
You see it, that disgust, in the tribunals of old men who
linger at the co-ops and country stores, men entitled
to a few, final years of repose on benches and cane-
back chairs after a lifetime of third shifts, stretch-outs,
and see-through sandwiches. Their bone-handled
knives, blades black with age and sharpened to paper-
thinness, would freeze over the whetstone when some
shirker lounged by. "Jest sorry," they would hiss and
scrape the blade across the stone.

One-armed men shoveled coal, slung slingblades,
and drove pulpwood trucks. One-legged men limped
across factory floors. A blind man sold candy and
chewing gum at the Calhoun County Courthouse, and

no one dared cheat him. You need not use foul language to damn a man here. Just say that a day's work would kill him, and you tore him down to the bald nothing.

At least that is how it was when there was more work here, when cotton covered the land, foundries burned orange into the night, and the machines, life-giving machines, could be heard for miles in the surrounding dark, through the third shift and into a new dawn.

That has been a while.

Sonny and Theresa Parker were paying off a red Pontiac, a Grand Prix, when the latest rumors of a shutdown and permanent layoff began to filter through the mill and the surrounding county, threatening so much more than their survival.

"To me, if a man works and tries as hard as he can, he might not have much but at least he's a man," said Sonny, an overhauler who is responsible for keeping the mill's machines running. "You ain't no lowlife. You can walk around with your head up, if you have work. That's what a mill is. It's hot, hard, dangerous work. And it's loud, and if you ain't careful, it'll get you.

"But it ain't when it's runnin' that it's scary. It's when it ain't."

———

Once, when they had gathered around the beds of their pickups in the mill parking lot, the stories had made them smile. They told tales of the eccentric mill boss,

Greenleaf, who liked to stroll his property in rubber wading boots and a dressing gown, and built an electric fence around his dining room table to shock the cats. They grinned about Squat Low Webb, who did a stint as a deputy sheriff and was prone to squat low when the shooting started. And they laughed out loud about Pop Romine, who never buttoned the side button of his overalls and scandalized the women, who rode the bus all the way to Chattanooga to eat chili and then rode it all the way back again, who left with every carnival that came to town, who was deaf as a concrete block, but would go into the mill where his sisters Ethel and Maxie worked, bite down on the spinning frame and, through some miracle of vibration, hear every word they said.

The past is safely done. So they went back to it, to the days when every wide place in the road had a red-brick mill, when well-dressed wives of mill owners handed silver dollars to raggedy children on Sunday afternoons, and trucks rolled through the village streets every Christmas, passing out free shoes and frozen turkeys. Once, they even had their own baseball teams, mill hands who took their practice swings with cigarettes burning in their lips went into second with spikes high and found something very close to glory in stadiums of red dirt and chicken wire.

Before, there was only the dirt. The red clay had been the crucible here, and it had broken generations. The people chopped other men's cotton, picked other

men's cotton, and lives vanished between rows of endless, lovely, hateful white. The most standing the poor
people could usually attain, when a landed man's name
was mentioned, was to say, "Oh, I picked for him."

Just one year after the Civil War finally ground to
its inevitable end, industrialists scouted the foothills
of Northeastern Alabama as a place for cotton mills,
especially along the Coosa River. But it was after 1900
before Yankee investors planned and constructed a
mill here, a thing of vast, echoing chambers, its towering ceilings held up by pillars taller than ships' masts.

The company promised houses, cast-iron heaters,
and coal. There would be a company store, a company
school, and a company church, and electric lights. All
this for a monthly rent of about twenty-five cents a room
for a three-room house. So they came walking, some
with everything they owned in a toe sack, some walking beside a wagon full of dirty-faced, hungry children.

It could not get so bad they would not want it.

The mill whistle, which blew for the first time in
October 1905, would open a new world to that exodus
of men, women, and barefoot urchins, who were especially prized by mill owners because their small, deli-
cate fingers could flutter inside machines without getting caught. Even into the 1930s, adult workers made
as little as seven dollars for a fifty-five-hour week. Pay
slips in its first twenty years show that, after rent and
food, workers routinely took home a monthly salary of
$0.00. But it was regular, life-sustaining work, and did

not depend on the fate of a blind, staggering mule, or the fickle nature of rain.

"I was fourteen years old when I went to work there. Why, that's not such a little girl," said Reba Houck, who was born in '24 and went to work on third shift in '38, after she planted, chopped, and picked cotton in her Daddy's field until twilight. "I was making fourteen dollars a week, twice as much as a grown man could make sharecropping. I bought me and my Momma and Daddy clothes. Back then, you see, it didn't matter about age."

Reba spent thirty-nine years in the mill.

"When I retired, Daddy took the Oldtimer's [Alzheimer's] and I sat with him until he passed in '89. I go to town now and see some of them, some of the old ones I worked with, but, darlin', I've forgot their names."

It was meant to be here, people said. The Great Depression had not killed it, or labor wars, or even World Wars, which took so many of the young men that the ones who did not serve were ashamed to look their neighbors in the face. It had even survived a direct hit by a massive tornado, an act of God. There had been layoffs, slow-downs and short-time, and even a closure or two, but it always reopened, always re-hired.

It held to people, even in death.

Iladean Deason Ford, who is well past seventy now, was six years old when she roamed the mill village, eating supper at a different house every night, whether she was invited or not. They lived at 7 A Street when her father began to show the early signs of brown lung. "I don't go down through there," she said, "I don't see my Daddy walking across the street."

The modern-day workers can tell you the year, month, and day they got on, the information stored away with birthdays and anniversaries and their babies' first words, but, somehow, more important. That is what they say, "got on," not hired, as if this were the last rung on a ladder, a high branch in a tree. It means they got someplace important, almost someplace safe.

"I got on September 20, 1974," said Smiley Sams. "I quit school when I was sixteen, and Momma said I could either go back to school or I could go to work. Momma worked here. I got nine brothers and sisters, and all but one worked here. I've never even filled out an application. This is all I've ever done."

He took his place on a line of machines that had spun enough yarn to tie the moon and earth together with one long, uninterrupted cotton string, on a floor worn smooth by people named Hop, Bunk, Chee, Slate Rock, Squirrely, Dago, Jutt, Hook, Kitty, Boss, Elk, Lefty, Possum, Sam Hill, Pot Likker, the Sandwich Thief, and the Clinker Man.

But by the year 2001, it was the future they talked about, an uncertain nothingness every bit as grim to them as the mill's darkest past.

———

They could have just left, all two hundred of them. The mill's last generation could have loaded everything they owned on a pickup and a flat-bed trailer, and said goodbye. They could have stopped at the mill office for one last paycheck, what they call "picking up their time." The Okies, when the winds blew the dust from beneath their feet, left their struggle behind. There is no shame in it. Sometimes, the road is all there is.

Two things held them here.

One, they did not know if another secure place was for their kind. It was as if once they picked up their time, their time would be over.

Two, they were bound, many of them, to these mountains with something longer and harder than nails or even chains. Few of them owned more than a few acres of the land they loved, and some of them, as their ancestors had, still went to sleep in rented houses. But the highway led no place they wanted to go.

Their ancestors had watered these trees with sweat, bile, and blood, not in some silly, philosophical way, but drop by drop. These dense canopies of oaks and pines had, for almost two hundred years, hidden hunger, hardship, violence, massacre, and murder— their story. But, as the old men like to say, they were *rar' purty trees.*

The mill paid the light bill, grocery bill, and the Christmas bill in a land where big buck deer leap across the blacktop, where canned peaches, apple butter, and crabapple jelly shine yellow-gold in the sunlight through the kitchen window, and nothing— not two cars parked side by side at a motel, not even their blood pressure —is a secret.

"You could get a job here if you wanted it," said Debbie Glenn, whose father farmed cotton in Calhoun County. She went to work in the Jacksonville mill as a young woman, and stayed. She considered it a blessing to wake up in this land. "I got to stay at home. The people I worked with became closer to me than my own family."

They considered themselves kin. The Reverend James Martin was born at 127 D Street and married a girl from 43 B Street, Sara Ford. They remember a village where people would give a fistfull of flour to co-workers, even if their fingernails scraped the bottom of their own sack. It was called a "grocery shower," the Reverend Martin said.

"If you got in trouble, people would help you out," said Sara Martin. But, "you didn't hear much complaining."

They took each other to the doctor, kept each other's children, and brought in a few hundred covered dishes for a mill dinner every Thanksgiving, Christmas, and Easter. Men discussed their gout in line at the funeral home, or on stadium benches under Friday night lights. Women discussed the sorry nature of men.

In time, they worked not just for subsistence, but for one of the best blue collar paychecks in their foothills. The modern-day workers, whose ancestors labored to stave off deprivation, made ten dollars an hour, eleven dollars, more, and bought modest houses, bass boats, and above-ground swimming pools. The mill here, like others around the country, became safer, cleaner, better ventilated. A job that had once carried a social stigma—lintheads, people called them—now carried a rock-solid respectability. And the thing the mill workers never could explain to better-off people was, it always had.

But human dignity, in a global economy, is just one more cost to cut. Long before the economic meltdown of 2008, the age of the textile worker was coming to an end.

In 1991, an American trade journal ran this advertisement:

Rosa Martinez produces apparel for U.S. markets on her sewing machine in El Salvador. You can hire her for thirty-three cents an hour.

———

A dying machine has a smell to it, an acrid, burning smell that tells you it is about to finish, as all mechanical things will, in a junked silence. It was Sonny Parker's job to know when a machine's life was coming to an end.

But in Jacksonville, in the winter of 2001, the oil on the machines still smelled new and clean. The company, even in its decline, had spent millions on the future of this one mill. Air blew through a brand-new air-conditioning system, and workers laid new, gleaming hardwood floors. It was like a written guarantee to Sonny and the others here, people who saved every left-over screw, washer, bent nail, and scrap of wire they had ever come across, just in case they might need it someday in some machine they did not yet even own. They could not conceive of such a waste, all this construction, on a doomed mill.

In the midst of the uncertainty, mill workers said, company officials told them that the cavernous structure was doing fine work, and their jobs were safe.

But mostly, Sonny trusted in the machines.

"Any time you look at brand new machines," he said, "you know the talk of shuttin' down is just talk."

Like most of the people here, he had cotton in his bloodstream even before he was born. He had worked in mills as a boy and man. He could say, without an ounce of exaggeration, that his mother died to make less money in a day than most well-off people left scattered on a restaurant table top. In her day, mill owners treated human components of their mills like so many interchangeable parts, and when one of them wore out, there was always another, fresh, new, and even cheaper part waiting to be plugged in.

His mother walked miles to a mill every afternoon for the second shift, and came home before midnight. "My dad was a bad alcoholic. They separated when I was six years old." His mother contracted brown lung early, and suffered. Early on, he understood what their living cost.

He helped as much as he could. He picked up pecans for money, and ran a paper route on his bicycle before going to school. "That's how we made our living, me and my Mom," he said. "At times we'd go to bed, nothing to eat but cornbread and buttermilk with salt and pepper. It was rough on Momma." To help the family get by, firemen at the station next door would cook extra food for them for lunch and supper, "'cause sometimes we didn't have anything," he said.

One day on his paper route, a car crashed into him. He was not badly hurt, but his bike was ruined. Insurance from the driver replaced his bike and gave him $150. "Back then, $150 was a lot of money," he said. "There was a dress my Mama had been wanting. I told her, 'You take that money and buy a new dress.' That's what she did."

His mother wore it as she was courted by a man at the mill, James Edward Harris, a good man who became his stepfather and treated him like his own son. Sonny likes to think the dress bought his mother a little happiness before she died. But that is how a cotton-mill story goes. There is always that trade, the mill giving something with one hand as, with the other, it takes something away.

———

To sleep at night, they had to ignore the bones.

In the wider world, they were already relics, left-over pieces of a rummage sale that was shipping their industry across borders, across oceans. The number of jobs in United States textile mills slipped from 2.3 million in 1970 to 1.6 million in 1996.

Almost as long as Sonny Parker had been a mill hand, the mills had been in decline, but there were so many across the Carolinas, across Alabama, that it seemed like a man could walk through the doors of one mill and step right into the door of another.

Like Twain's Tom Sawyer, he had seen his own funeral. Economists told him and his co-workers that their jobs were not good jobs, not jobs of the future, told them, with straight faces, they should retrain for jobs in computer programming, radiology, or hotel management. They heard industrialists, men who had never pulled a wrench, say that the workers who talked about keeping American jobs in America were ignorant of global economics, of the big picture. But it seemed to the men and women of the mills that global economics was a rich man's phrase and a rich man's invention, and the big picture was a sure place for a little man to lose himself for good.

In 1994, in the midst of that steady decline, President Clinton signed the North American Free Trade Agreement, NAFTA, which promised to be a boon to an already struggling American working class by, somehow, creating a greater demand for American

goods. Instead, American jobs poured south to third-
world plants where workers drew drinking water from
ditches and lived in squatter communities beside hast-
ily constructed industrial parks that stank of open
sewers and human suffering. It had seemed, to even
the most unlettered working man, such a fool's bargain,
a governmental gutting of the industry in a time when
it was already dying. At first it was Latin America, then
China that swallowed the American textile industry.

Here, the closing of doors boomed across the state,
and layoffs rolled on and on. "Skeletons, all over Alabama," said Harvey Jackson, head of the history department at Jacksonville State University, just up the
hill from the cotton mill village.

In 1997, it was Johnson Industries in Valley. The
plant shut down and laid off more than three hundred
workers. Four years later, Russell Yarns shut down
four plants in Coosa County, Sylacauga and two in Al-
exander City, putting eight hundred out of work. CMI
in Geneva padlocked its doors, leaving four hundred
without work. The graveyard extended far beyond
Alabama, to the Carolinas, Georgia, Arkansas, Tennessee, and up into Maine, Rhode Island, Pennsylva-
nia. Hundreds of thousands of workers were left with
nothing, with no health insurance, with just scraps of
pensions or no pensions at all.

In Jacksonville, the workers watched their own
company's decline with a kind of sickening disbelief.
Fruit of the Loom shut down mills across the South,

and laid off thousands. The last time the looms of the country had been so quiet was in the Great Textile Strike of 1934, when mill workers nationwide banded together to protest deplorable pay and dangerous, unhealthy conditions. The machines went silent that time because the workers demanded basic human rights and something more than starvation pay, and they battled strike busters and the National Guard in the streets. Thousands of them were tear-gassed, jailed and beaten, some clubbed to death or crippled by hired thugs in what would become the bloodiest, government-sanctioned reaction to a labor movement in United States history. But the spindles started up again, eventually, because the workers were still necessary.

This time, machines were dismantled, crated, and moved. Towns withered. Shoe stores became pawn shops. Chain groceries that had carried name-brand foods became places to buy unlabeled, dented mystery cans, twenty cents a chance.

Hundreds of thousands went without work and health insurance, with house and car payments and grocery bills unmet. These were not a people who wanted federal aid. They wanted a tool to pound out a living, but their hammers—the machines—were being pulled away.

But not here, not yet. The Jacksonville mill roared on. People prayed that it would, in places like Pleasant Valley, Roy Webb, Williams, Piedmont, Midway, Nances Creek, Websters Chapel, White Plains, Whites

Gap, Hollis Crossroads, Tredegar, Cedar Springs, Blue Mountain, Alexandria, Rabbit Town, Frogtown, and through the West Side.

"Every time we were told to do a budget, I just prayed that we could get the cost down low enough to stay open," said Gail Penny, the mill's office manager and accounting manager for twenty-six years. "I'd say, 'Lord, let this be it.'"

But people did more than pray. To save themselves, they increased production and worked safe. They believed in an old-fashioned ideal, that by working long, fast, and hard enough, by making something fine and making more of it in less time, they could force the men in suits to see their value, and reward them with work.

"People killed themselves on them machines," Sonny said.

When machines wore out, the overhaulers rebuilt them from the floor up, racing the clock. Sonny started spending more time at the mill than he did at home. There were his wife's medical bills to pay, so he took as much overtime as they would give him, volunteering to work Saturdays and Sundays, too.

Saturdays paid time and a half time, and Sundays paid double time.

"I'd go in for twelve and get paid for twenty-four," he said. "You can't beat that."

Routinely, he worked sixteen hours a day, seven days a week.

"I told him, 'You might as well put your bed down there because you spend more time there than you do at home,'" Theresa said. "And I told him, 'You might as well have your funeral down there, too.'" But in that surrounding silence, the roar was music. Here, you could put your hands against the side of the red-brick mill, day and night, and feel it hum.

The gossipers said this time it wasn't enough, that this time the company really would shut them down, and all of it, their pay, their insurance, would vanish. But the company told them no, their jobs were safe, said Sonny and other workers here.

"It was hope people was reaching out for," said Delorise Keith. "They made us believe."

Benny Buse, a fifty-one-year-old head overhauler, reassured the workers under him as his bosses reassured him. "People were buying things left and right," he said.

Two bosses told Sonny his job was so safe he could buy a house, a new car.

"Aint nothin' to this shuttin,' down," one boss told him.

"Just people runnin' their mouths," another boss claimed.

"They told me I could retire here," Sonny said.

If all it took were guts and muscle, they would run these brand-new machines into smoke and washers.

They believed it on the loading docks, where the air smelled like hot brakes and diesel fuel, where eighteen wheelers brought in thousands of tons of ginned, dirty-white cotton. The tow motors did not crawl across the docks but raced. They believed it in the opening room, where men armored as if they were going to war cut the bands off five hundred-pound bales, so many, so fast that it sounded like a never-ending volley of artillery. They believed it as they pushed cotton with their naked hands at machines designed to grab, chop, and fluff with spinning steel blades, blades that could slice a wrench in two. They believed it at the carding machines, where the separated cotton became a fat coil of yarn, and in the spinning room, where those coils were spun into thinner, tougher threads. They believed it in the office, in the break rooms, and in the parking lot, where men gathered around new and like-new pickups and cars, nothing fancy, just proof of their optimism, their faith.

Sonny and Theresa bought a new car, the red Pontiac.

"We can go anywhere in the world in that, baby," he said.

———

Theresa sings about heaven in a way that makes you wonder if she has already seen it. She was two when she started singing in church, so little that her grandfather, the Rev. Huse Garmon, had to hold her up high, so people could see her. "I could sing before I talked," Theresa said.

Her daddy, Donald, also a veteran of the mills, played guitar and sang in a group that traveled from camp meetings to Indian reservations to high school gymnasiums, delivering the gospel with a little music, to make it go down easier. Her family formed its own group, the Garmon Family, and was famous in the little churches and brush arbors. Their signature song was "The Eastern Gate." Theresa sang the high notes, and her mother, Nancy, used to smile at how long her baby girl could hold them in the air.

Then He whispers 'peace,' be still now
and the winds must obey
Then burdens are lifted away

But their bread always came from the mills. Sonny got on at the Jacksonville mill in '74. She followed him inside three years later. She will never forget that first day, and the mist. She walked into a room that seemed filled with gnats, a swarm of white.

There were no warnings, she said. Few people wore masks.

That first year, she was in the hospital with pneumonia. "I'd never had any trouble with my lungs before then," she said. She missed so much work—more than ninety days —she automatically lost her job. The mill rehired her, but in one year she developed pneumonia twice more. "Antibiotics is about all I got," she said. She would be bed ridden, get better, and return to the mill. "It kept getting worse and worse and worse."

Sonny stood helpless, watching his mother's story

play out, again.

He asked her not to go in sick.

"She was working herself to death," Sonny said.

Theresa knew. Like Sonny, she had seen this tragedy before in her own mother.

"Mama worked for sixteen years in the winding room of a mill, a mill with no kind of filters," Theresa said. "The doctors kept asking, 'How long has she smoked?' But she didn't smoke."

On a Thursday morning in February 2001, Theresa woke coughing and fighting for air. "Do I need to take you to the doctor?" Sonny asked.

"No," she said.

She had coughed through the morning before.

Later that morning, her daughter called. Theresa could not lift it, but knocked the phone off its hook. All her daughter heard was moaning. Theresa's mother went to her door, knocked, and then started to beat it. She called Sonny at the mill and told him he needed to come home. They found her on the floor, barely breathing, burning with fever. They rushed her to the hospital, where doctors found her heart was racing and her potassium levels had dropped dangerously low. She was unconscious for two days.

Her doctor told her she almost quit breathing and that if her family hadn't rushed her in when they did, she would be dead. "They ran all kinds of tests because they were afraid I had brain damage," she said. "I went so long without oxygen."

After going in the hospital in February 2001, "the lung doctor wouldn't let me go back in the mill. [Mill managers] called me and said there wasn't nothing they could give me. They said they were sorry. I killed myself for twenty-one years. I looked like a skeleton with skin over it."

She has permanent damage in her lungs. To breathe, she uses a nebulizer four times a day and inhalers charged with medicine. "I still have bad days," she said. "My lungs will never get any better. It limits the things you can do. You can't run with your grandkids like you should. I used to mop the whole floor."

She sings, still, but it is different now. In December of 2004, Theresa and her father sang at a small concert outside Jacksonville. . Her father is blind now, but still plays guitar, "can still whup the fire out of it," she said. About fifty people gathered, eating hot dogs, chili, and hand-scooped ice cream. The Garmons sang their standard, the one the people always asked for.

If you hasten off to glory
Linger near the Eastern Gate
For I'm coming in the morning
So you'll not have long to wait

The high notes died in her chest.

———

Sonny and a crew of overhaulers were working on a stalled machine in March, 2001, when they saw their boss moving toward them across the floor.

"He was running," Sonny said.

"Well," the boss said, "it's true."

It happened every day, these rumors.

It peeled the skin off a man.

Sonny just went back to work.

"Get out of here," he said. "We're trying to do our job."

floria's dollar

She does not talk a lot. When she does, her stories
are plain and small. Her story, for sixty years, was
written in books that had no words, only numbers,
of the miles of yarn she spun. It is rich people, usually, who live on in biographies, in the pages of the
social register. Working people live on in ledgers.
The idea that anyone would want to know about
that, about such a life, puzzles her. "It was all there
was," said Floria Fortenberry. "I'd do it again, if it
was all there was."

Yet there is, deep in her past, a small legend, not
from the mill, but the cotton itself. When she was in
her thirties, standing at the start of an endless row of
cotton, she told a boss man she could do a thing he
said could not be done, and raced the hands of his
watch for a single dollar bill.

Floria never called it a legend.

It was just something that happened one day, in
the red dirt.

Like a lot of people here in the foothills, her life
was bound to cotton from the start. She was born just
before the Great Depression, as men in suits flung
themselves from windows on Wall Street, and picked
her first cotton before she could see over the stalks. "I

was six, that first time," she said. She was Floria Wright then, and picked beside her mother and father, Minnie and Jim, on their small farm.

She married Clayton Fortenberry on December 27, 1944, when she was seventeen, and they had three children. Clayton worked construction and factory jobs, and Floria worked in the mills in Blue Mountain and Jacksonville, to help out.

She did not pick cotton for a living then, in the 1960s. She did it to make a few extra dollars for school clothes or baby clothes or little luxuries. "I wanted my kids to go as nice as anybody," she said. "Once, I made enough to cover a couch."

The people who know her, members of her church, say she is a fine person who reads her Bible and lives it. She does not need a legend, even a small one, to mark her time on this earth, any more than she needs a big car, or a gaudy hat.

"We were tough, I guess," is about the most she will say. Then, for just a second or two, a disease in her lungs—caused by asbestos—takes her breath away. People who know her say a bad cold can almost kill her.

"I am smothering, I believe," she said. "Sometimes I need prayer."

But she hates to complain.

"Just don't put nothin' in there," she said, "that'll make my children ashamed of me. We've come a long way since then."

It happened in the middle 1960s, at the end of an

era—an era not fading into antiquity so much as it was being gnawed away. The big, mechanical pickers, like giant, chewing pests, had arrived in the red-dirt fields of the foothills, tearing through the fields, leaving the cotton dirty and half picked, ripped into scrap. Pickers of flesh and blood, seasonal workers who picked to make a little extra cash, were obsolete. The future ran on diesel, and it didn't even pick clean.

———

Floria was one of the best, the fastest. Her hands moved in a rhythm, one reaching for one open boll as the other, in a smooth mechanical motion, eased another boll into the sack. She could pick three hundred pounds in just one day in a time when some people were glad to pick one hundred, and her cotton was clean, without twigs and brittle leaf. When you sighted down a row she had picked it was green-black, empty, without a scrap of white.

Her mind, when she picked, was free of daydreams.

"I thought of the money," she said.

She did not think about washing machines and new bedroom suites and kitchen tables. She thought about that little bit extra, a boy's shirt, or boots, or a notebook. She liked to crochet when she was sitting down, because otherwise it was just wasted time, and as she picked she would calculate how much yarn she might buy, and what she might make with it.

"A dollar," she said, "was a whole lot."

She concentrated on stripping every stalk clean,

on filling her sack the fullest in the least amount of steps—one boll, a million times.

"I thought about making all I could."

But no matter how careful you were, it would always stick you. She would reach for a soft, white boll of cotton only to feel the bur, a needle-like sticker on the nut-like shell, lance her fingers or slip under the quick of her fingernails.

"They would break off under the skin," she said.

You seldom quit long enough to dig them out. Some of the old women would carry a sewing needle stuck in their bonnets, or a big safety pin on the collar of their dresses, and at the noon break or at quttin' time they would gently try to lift them out.

"It'd fester if you didn't," Floria said.

It could be burning hot in the afternoon, but picking time came as the summer was dying, and in the gloom of the early mornings a cold dew soaked the fields.

"You worked wet, up to your neck," she said, "and cold."

The dew made the bolls slick, and made her sure, deft fingers clumsy. "My hands would bleed," she said.

The pickers gathered discarded guano sacks at the side of the field and piled and burned them. "It was the only way we could warm our hands," she said.

Snakes, Copperheads and rattlers, hid in the stalks. The wasps and yellow jackets came out of holes in the red dirt, and the old women would daub a little wet snuff on the sting, to ease it. The cotton stank of poison.

The mill workers could even smell it in the bales.

But sometimes the cotton was so tall it seemed as if she barely had to bend over to fill a sack, and she and her friends would find a watermelon vine, a gift, in the field, and they would break it open right there and eat it with their hands.

The farmers paid a sliding scale, from a handful of change in the worst of times—in the Depression, the people worked for what they could get—to two dollars for one hundred pounds in the 1950s and early 1960s. To ease the tug of the sack, some workers daydreamed about a better life, not some great wealth on earth but something finer, everlasting. Old women sang about it as they dragged their sacks across the clay.

I heard an old, old story
How the Savior came from Glory
How he gave his life on Calvary
To save a wretch like me

Flora did not sing as she worked, but she listened. The songs swirled around her and over her, with a sweetness that cut the dust and kept the devil of self-pity and laziness underground.

Oh victory in Jesus,
My Savior forever
He sought me, and bought me
With His redeeming Blood

Some people prayed as they picked. Beatrice Mc-Curley, a big woman who would get so full of the spirit in church that she would shake the hair pins from her head, would straighten up in the rows and begin to speak to Jesus in the rising dust.

No one was quite sure what to do then, in the middle of a field, when a woman was getting right with God.

"She'd just break out praying, and we stopped and listened," Floria said.

> *He loved me 'ere I knew Him*
> *All my love is due Him*
> *And plunged me to victory*
> *Beneath the cleansing flood*

———

The big truck came to get them in early morning. At the field, they climbed out into a chill, moisture beading on the bolls. The air always smelled of snuff and Juicy Fruit and the lunches they carried to the field in brown-paper bags: fried bologna sandwiches with mustard, leftover biscuits filled with cold potatoes and fatback, peanut butter and saltine crackers. A few sipped cold coffee from glass jars and fed their babies from bottles full of diluted canned milk.

The old women picked in impractical dresses—they owned no pants, considering such dress un-Christian—and carried yesterday's wounds on their shins, fine, razor-like slashes of the briars, now dried into thin, red lines. They wore bonnets and used wooden ice cream spoons to fill their lips with snuff before they slung on their sack. Old men rolled one last cigarette. They smoked it down to a nub, wet their thick fingers and pinched it out, leaving the shreds of paper and tobacco to blow through the field.

The younger women, like Floria, picked in pants and sneakers and wore long sleeves to keep stalks and burs from cutting them up. She always picked beside her friend and sister-in-law, Jewel, sometimes with their children. But on this day the children were in school, leaving Floria and Jewel unencumbered.

That day, the sun rose on a field owned by a farmer named Naugher, an honest, hard-working man who never acted as if he was better than them. He did not sit in the shade or the cab of his truck, figuring his profits. He picked in the cotton beside them. He paid two dollars for every one hundred pounds, the going rate, and some of them would work all day for that.

This field was different from others they picked. Its rows went on, it seemed, for miles. Naugher called the pickers around him to give them their sacks, and to make them a promise that, in all the years men and women had picked his field, he had never had to keep.

"I don't expect y'all to finish a row and back," Naugher told them. "But if y'all can finish one row out there and back, before quitting time, I'll pay y'all a dollar extry."

The pickers didn't say a word. It was like being promised a slice of the moon if you could knock it down with a rock.

Then Floria, perhaps the most quiet among them, spoke up.

"I can do that," she said.

She did not mean it to sound like bragging; it's just that ideas are not real, maybe, until you hang them on the air.

She weighed one hundred pounds, more or less, and worked chest-high in even short cotton.

Naugher had seen big men fail, men who moved as if they had wheels under them, and picked as if they had three arms.

"No," Naugher said to her, not mean, just matter of fact. "You can't."

He turned and walked away.

Jewel looked at her friend.

"Floria, we can't…"

"Yes, we can," Floria said.

They entered the field about six thirty, side by side.

Quitting time was when Naugher said it was.

They worked fast and steady. It did no good to rush faster than their hands could strip the bolls so their hands had to fly over the stalks to keep pace with their feet. They barely talked. They ate cornbread and buttermilk at dinner, the noon meal, stopping just a few minutes. By the afternoon, Jewel was already bone weary, trying to keep up. Sweat soaked them. Red dust and black specks of trash, from the stalks, slicked their faces.

If Floria was hurting, or exhausted, it was invisible to Jewel.

"I can't do no more," she said.

"Come on," Floria said.

She dragged her friend along by force of will.

They made the turn in the early afternoon and headed back. By late afternoon, the cotton wagon still looked like a toy on the horizon.

The light was dimmer now.

"We...won't...never..." Jewel said.

"Come on."

The other pickers watched from behind them.

They did not cheer. This was work, and they did not cheer work.

Naugher watched, a puzzled look on his face.

Who would kill themselves, for one dollar?

"Slow down," he yelled across the rows.

At about four-thirty, the two women staggered up to the cotton wagon.

Naugher did not say a word, just weighed them in.

"There was just this look on his face," Jewel said, "like he still didn't believe."

The scale spun to the truth of it. The two women, together, had picked more than six hundred pounds of cotton—at two dollars per one hundred pounds, they made six dollars each, and a little change. They had picked more than three times their weight.

Floria had picked 329 pounds, "the most I ever picked."

Naugher peeled two more dollars off his roll, and gave it to them.

He still did not say anything, at least not that anyone can recall.

But they did catch him smiling.

When they had all weighed in, the pickers climbed back on the big truck and rode it out of the field. When Floria got home there were clothes to wash and children to hush, and supper to fix. The dollar vanished, as all money does.

———

The machines took over the fields, steel arms spinning, threshing, their mechanical mouths sucking the cotton up in big gulps. The pick sacks rotted in the barns.

But the lives of the people of the foothills were still wrapped in cotton, in the mills of Jacksonville, Piedmont, Blue Mountain, Leesburg, other small towns and wide places in the road.

Not just anyone could do this work, and some people didn't last a day. The machines snatched the hair from some peoples' heads, ripped the clothes off bodies, and did worse—not every day, but enough to scare the timid people away.

Floria was not frightened by the machines. She worked steady, smart, and without accident. Her mind did not drift. It focused on the work. Disaster waited, for the dreamers.

The poet Ron Rash wrote of it:
Lost wages or lost fingers
The risk of reflection

"I saw a man get his fingers cut off," she said. "I been tryin' to think of his name. They picked 'em up, put 'em in a can."

She ignored the heat. "It was hot, real hot," she said of the mill, "but you can get used to anything."

She got used to the noise, like a million gnashing metal teeth, and the vibration, which shook the sweat from her face.

It was hard, though, to breathe the white air, "and you could smell the poison in it, sometimes," she said.

There was always cotton in the air, a fine mist. "You couldn't help but breathe it," she said. "I'd pull strings of cotton from my eyes, from my nose." But the workers would almost smother when it was time to clean the machines. They used air hoses to blow the excess cotton away, but that meant blowing it into the air. Often, the bosses would have the workers go back to work immediately, in that suffocating mess. "Oh Lord, it was bad in that card room," she said. "But there was this one manager who was good to us. He let us stop while they blowed off."

"They never told us nothin', that it would hurt us," she said, "and I am not one to go to the doctor."

She seems more concerned that her feet hurt.

"Never could find a shoe that fit," she said.

———

She retired in Jacksonville in 1991, to watch grand-
babies play, to draw a breath that was not timed by a
clock. In 1997, at a free screening for respiratory disease at a Holiday Inn, she found out she had a lung disease linked to her years of work.

But like so many of the women and men who have
been hurt by the conditions of the place, she refuses to
shake her fist at it, to wish it never happened.

She remembers one paycheck in particular.

"I went to Sears," she said, "and got a dining room
suite. It was a big table with six chairs, padded chairs,
with vinyl."

———

Jewel keeps the little legend from vanishing.

"I tell my grandchildren about it," said Jewel, who
is in her sixties now. "We did something they said we
couldn't."

She was driving through the county with her
grandbaby, Kay Lynn, when the little girl saw a cotton field.

"Mawmaw, what is that?" she asked.

"I stopped and let her walk to the edge of the field,"
Jewel said.

The little girl reached out and touched the boll.
The bur jabbed her hand.

"It sticks you," she said.

It made Jewel think of Floria, how she could move
so fast down the rows. It was not that she did not feel

the sticker slide into her fingers. The secret to it was always in knowing that it would hurt you, and you reached for it anyway.

———

The fields do not blanket the valleys anymore, but that only makes the fields that remain seem even lovelier. The cotton is tall, bolls fat and bursting. Floria passes them on the way to her doctor's office. She doubts she could pick a puny 100 pounds of it, let alone that legendary 329.

"I would like to pick," she said, "one more time."

She does not think about her legend much. But once in a while, she comes across it among other frivolous things, like an odd, leftover piece of knitting yarn, or a button that doesn't match anything she wears. You can't make anything with it. And what is a story worth?

the kingdom

He lived in a mansion not far from the village so he could hear his mill run, and if one of those Southern peckerwoods went slack or made trouble, even for a minute, he put them out the gate, put them out of their company-owned house. Some people say he did a lot of good for this little town, that he gave away shoes and Christmas hams, and, while he paid these poor mountain people almost nothing, it was still the most they ever had. But ask the old people in the mill village if William Ivan Greenleaf was better or worse than others of his kind, and they just smile. That, they say, is like sticking your arm inside a box of copperheads, and feeling around for the best one.

——

The mill hands heard him coming as they trudged to work in the pre-dawn, their steps sending up puffs of ash from streets paved with cinders from the mill's coal-fired generator. A massive twelve-cylinder engine pounded the air around them, as if anything to do with Greenleaf was large, loud, and mean, and bug-eyed headlights, big as searchlights on a prison wall, stabbed out from the gleaming chrome. And there he would be, riding like a sultan in a long, black Packard touring sedan. The sedan did not stop for cats or dogs or people, who learned to step off into the weeds when the car went by. They stood in the ditch till it passed, greasy, brown-paper sacks in their hands. It was the same lunch, every day, white-bread sandwiches made from pink potted meat, spread so thin the color almost didn't show on the bread.

The big man did not wave or nod or look their way, just lounged in that leather as the big car wheeled into the gates of his kingdom. The best-dressed man in Alabama, people said, a high-toned New Hampshire Episcopalian in spats and a Bowler hat, teeth grinding on a Blackstone cigar. He was six foot two, barrel chested and hawk nosed, his iron-gray hair in a perfect part straight down the middle of his arrogant head. As he stomped into the office, clerks and secretaries smiled or tipped their hats and said, "Good morning, sir," but he usually just walked on by. "He walked and stood like he was the king," said Homer Barnwell, whose father and mother worked in Greenleaf's mill. "He played the part. He was the part."

A lot of people hated him, but never so much as in '33. A new president, Franklin D. Roosevelt, signed legislation that made child labor and starvation wages illegal in the textile mills. Greenleaf, who paid the lowest wages in Calhoun County, smirked at the new national minimum of twelve dollars a week, and thumbed his nose at what he called the "damned socialists." Rather than offer his workers, who made seven dollars a week, a raise to a legal wage, he offered a compromise. He offered twenty-five cents more a week.

The resentment that had burned for years inside the walls of the gnashing, roaring mill finally roiled out into the streets, just as the sweat-soaked first shift was staggering home. They gathered in the tiny yards and in the alphabet streets in a dank, hot August dusk, hard men and hard women, cotton still clinging to them like moss. There were no grand speeches, at least none that anyone can remember. Men waved pistols and axe handles and passed jars of clear liquor from hand to hand. Torches lit up A, B, C, and D streets, and even now old people talk about it, those streets of fire.

Finally, when the people were mad enough, they went after their tormenter. They fetched Greenleaf from a closet and bore him to Big Spring, to the hanging tree. He didn't seem to weigh all that much for a big shot, and they slung him from man to man like a rag doll as they cursed, laughed, and hooted. When they slipped the rope over his head the crowd screamed, and women in faded flower-print dresses pushed children behind them, so they could not see. A few yards away a squad car idled in the grass, but the officers knew better than to get between these hill people and their vengeance, so they just let them be.

In the glow of a hundred torches, they raised him high, their scarred arms and mutilated fingers his gallows. His face was covered with a toe sack, but they hung a sign around his neck so everyone would know:

GREENLEAF

Then they let him drop.

The roar reached up the hill, to the square, beyond.

People in town, gentler people, stared down at them, a little afraid.

It got quiet then, quickly.

The torches and hatred spent, the people shuffled home in the dark.

"They left him up there a good while," said Homer Barnwell, who was a little boy then.

The people disappeared inside their little houses, to suppers of cornbread and beans. But it helped a little, what they had done.

It gave their hatred a place to swing.

But how truly satisfying can it be, to hang a tyrant of rags and straw?

————

Greenleaf was not born to power, but took to it. He owned an interest in the mill through his wife, Frances. Charles Buck Henry, a scion of timber and railroad barons and a childhood friend, gave Frances thirty thousand dollars in mill stock as a wedding gift. At the time, Greenleaf was in Milwaukee, running an ironworks. He had no experience in the textile industry, but Henry promised him a twenty-four thousand dollar salary—a small fortune then—and an unlimited expense account to lure him to Alabama. The still-new mill was not profitable, and Greenleaf was hired to make it so. He came down from New Hampshire in 1911 and became not so much a mill boss, people here say, as a feudal lord.

It was his prerogative, their hunger, their deprivation, their life and death. People still talk about
Frank Watson, who was ordered up a ladder to reat-
tach a disconnected electric cable on May 10, 1917. The
mill bosses would not shut down power and halt production, even for a minute. So, as one of his bosses
stood below, telling him to get on with it, he joined a
dead line to a live one and the current burned him to
death against the side of the building. Maggie Watson, his widow, sued the mill, but lawyers for Greenleaf argued, successfully, that Watson died of his own
negligence, that he should have known better. But the
workers here knew the truth of it. Watson only did as
he was told, because to ignore an order was to forfeit
your job.

Others perished more slowly, choking on the
cotton they breathed in the unventilated, oven-like
rooms. The mangling of fingers, hands, and arms was
routine. The plant kept no records of such things, so
there are no statistics, only grim memory. But you do
not imagine a missing hand.

Yet in that disdain for the people who served him,
Greenleaf really was no better or worse than a hundred
others, no more oblivious to suffering. They forgive
him—even the worst of the tragedies—as a fact of life.
There was a Greenleaf everywhere there was a mill.

"As many times as I went down to that house, I
never did go inside," said Homer Barnwell, who grew

up with Greenleaf's children and played with one of
his sons, Russell. "Me and Russell went to school together. We were good buddies." He cannot explain,
exactly, why he always stopped beneath the columns.
"I don't know if they told me I couldn't go in. I just
knew I wasn't supposed to."

But the power Greenleaf held over them seemed
to swell, somehow, as the Great Depression settled on
the town, and he did things that made no more sense
than a small boy salting worms. He let their company
houses rot down around them, would try to cheat
workmen out of a dollar, for the sport of it, and was so
arrogant he believed that he got to say where the sun
should hang in the sky.

———

To carve away outside interference on how the mill
was run, Henry and Greenleaf reduced the board of
directors from eleven to three and installed Greenleaf
as vice president, superintendent and, most impor-
tantly, bookkeeper. The mill continued to report little profit, on paper, but Greenleaf grew wealthier. That
prompted minority stockholders to demand to see
company books. "Greenleaf refused to deliver said papers…and refused to allow the auditor to make exam-
ination of said papers," stated a lawsuit filed by the minority stockholders. Greenleaf, after losing his appeal
in the Alabama Supreme Court, just bought the stockholders out so he could run the mill as he pleased. The
Henry family still held financial power over him and

his mill, but to the working people here, Greenleaf was the monarch of the mill.

He made money even as the Depression began to squeeze and starve the people of the foothills. As people here lost everything they had, as banks foreclosed on farms, family homes, and timberland, Greenleaf was collecting deeds.

John Pruett, a young man then, was Greenleaf's next-door neighbor and friend.

But any rose-colored glasses he used to peer at his friend shattered a long time ago.

"Back then, Greenleaf was the only one buying things," said Pruett, who can still hear the bombast in Greenleaf's voice. "Nobody else had any money…and he didn't think much of you if you didn't."

Pruett, who had gotten to know the patriarch through the Greenleaf children, found that he was somehow acceptable to the old man. He was not a mill worker's child—his father ran the county retirement home—and he was welcome inside the Greenleaf home. In a time of prohibition and starvation, there was good bourbon at the Greenleaf table, and Friday night dances in the dining room. Greenleaf waltzed with the teenage sweethearts and friends of his sons, and, John Pruett said, liked to pat the young ladies on their derrieres. He would tell Pruett, as he left on a date, to "think of ol' man Greenleaf" if he got to second base.

A biplane pilot who dusted crops and barnstormed

around the South, Pruett had stories to tell of daring loops and deadly crashes, and as he got older the two of them sat alone, just drinking, talking. "He was a colorful old bastard," Pruett said. But in time, he would see the man sitting across from him on the veranda as cold, uncaring.

"I felt sorry for the people," said Pruett, who sometimes toured the mill with Greenleaf. "They didn't even have a break for lunch," and ate standing at their machines. "It was filthy. The latrines were stinking and dirty." Greenleaf did extend credit, he said, so that his employees could eat, but they labored in perpetual debt. "What the company took out ate up their paycheck," Pruett said. Greenleaf called it good business.

He saw himself as a benevolent soul who gave the poor mountain people a good life. But Greenleaf never bothered to repair any of the mill village houses, Pruett said. "I don't know how many he ruined," Pruett said. When a tenant confronted Greenleaf, he ordered them from his presence with these words: "When it is raining, I can't fix it, and when the sun is shining, it doesn't need it."

If you knocked heads with him, you lost. Since the days of the Creek Indian Wars, a pristine watering hole called Big Spring had provided a constant source of cold, sweet water to the town. Greenleaf, who owned property near the spring, fouled it with construction, and pumps and spigots in the town and mill village belched red mud. Greenleaf told the complainers they could go to hell, or see his lawyer.

He dealt routinely in thousands of dollars yet seemed to enjoy the tiniest confrontations. After a handyman named Luke finished a repair at the mansion, Greenleaf pulled out a wad of money and thumbed off a few bills. As he counted, he told Luke to carry a ladder to the garage and come back and get his pay.

Luke returned and asked for his money, and Greenleaf responded that he had already paid him. When Luke insisted he hadn't been paid, Greenleaf looked at Luke's helper. "You look like an honest sort of chap. I paid him, didn't I?"

The helper shook his head: "No, sir, you got your money out, but you didn't pay him."

"Well, I'll just pay you again, Luke," Greenleaf said.

"No, sir, you won't be paying me again," Luke replied. "You'll be paying me for the first time."

Greenleaf did not seem to understand what the work meant to them, the value they held for their own labor.

"He would do petty things," Pruett said. "My Uncle Bob almost shot Greenleaf once. Caught him moving a fence, stealing a couple of feet on a property line."

In this time of economic agony, he wasted thousands. Once, a crew delivered trees and dug more than one hundred holes for an orchard. "He never planted the first tree," Pruett said. "The holes are still there."

Another time, he had timber cut from land in nearby

White Plains. For days, trucks rolled into the yard with loads of raw lumber that hadn't been planed. Greenleaf stacked the lumber. "About forty thousand dollars worth of damn lumber rotted to the ground," Pruett said. "I've seen him waste so much money. God."

Greenleaf filled his yard with cars, and let many of them rot and rust, because he did not want anyone else to have them. He was eccentric, complicated, but more than anything, confident of his place in the world he had created. As sunset approached one evening, Pruett watched Greenleaf step off a certain distance from the dining room table and then do a hard left face. He looked through a piece of smoked glass at the setting sun and checked his watch. One of Greenleaf's sons explained, quietly, that Daddy Greenleaf believed the sun was off course.

In the mill village, he controlled the electricity, the water, the groceries, all of it. Even though he was a hard-drinking man, he did not want his workers to drink—that could get in the way of production. "There was a bootlegger down here then," Homer Barnwell said. "Greenleaf didn't like it. He hired a man from Birmingham to run him off. They shot each other."

He expected his employees to shop only at the company store with their metallic script, tokens called "clinkers." But Greenleaf also owned Westside Drug, a pharmacy, said Sam Stewart Sr., who was friends with Greenleaf's children. "He had them with food, and he had them with medicine," Stewart said.

The holidays brought out a gentler side of Green-leaf. Trucks would roll through the village, loaded with free shoes, hams, and turkeys. Yet he was insulted when working class people came accidentally into his presence. Two blue-collar boys from Piedmont came up his driveway in a rusty car, wanting to rent one of Greenleaf's houses. "Hell, by the time he got through insulting them, they just got in the car and left and blew the horn all the way out to the road," Pruett said. Greenleaf marched down the road after them, screaming about lawsuits.

But in a time of grim deprivation, when the whole world seemed worn and faded, Greenleaf exploded with color, with bombast and bluster.

Pruett remembers seeing Greenleaf walking through the yard one evening in his dressing gown and a pair of rubber boots.

Pruett yelled: "Good evening, Mr. Greenleaf."

"Who goes there?"

"John Pruett."

"Well, ol' John Pruett, where you going?"

"Goin' over to see ol' man Greenleaf."

"What are you going to see ol' man Greenleaf about?"

"I'm goin' over there to borrow a couple hundred dollars."

"Why you damn pauper," Greenleaf said, "you wouldn't know what to do with it if I gave it to you."

If Greenleaf was afraid of anything, it was his own government. Greenleaf told anyone who would listen that the Democrats were Communists in thin disguise, that putting them in power in Washington would be the end of everything American.

In 1932, he was confident that his America would not be so foolish and talked about all the big things he was going to do, in his empire, when the Republicans won the election. Then Franklin D. Roosevelt ruined everything.

Democrats meant reformers, and reformers meant unions, and unions meant that the little people would try to stand up to the big people, and this could not be allowed.

———

In 2004, in a sickroom in Jacksonville, Gardner Greenleaf whispered a defense of his father over the hiss of a respirator. But even as he lay dying of emphysema, his family still shaped the face of this town. He had recently sold fifty acres of Greenleaf land, some of the last, to developers of a new subdivision.

"But any damn thing we ever owned," he said, "it cost us."

His father, he said, should be remembered as a good man who treated workers humanely, paid them fairly, and created a safe, clean work environment. His father made sure that the mill store sold groceries and other items at cost. He said his father gave a doctor land for his home in return for providing medical services. "It didn't cost the cotton mill people one dime."

His father thought so much of his secretary at the

mill, Marie, that he named the children's fox terrier after her, spelling it backwards. "Eiram."

"It was a nice mill," he said. "It didn't have any problems."

His father fought to do away with the entrenched practice of child labor, he said, treated black and white employees the same in a time of rigid, violent segregation, and did not allow floor bosses to employ the hated "stretch-out," when machines ran so fast that people could not keep up and sometimes collapsed, exhausted, into their machines.

When he was a boy, he liked to watch it run, to watch the people rush across the floor. "It was beautiful," he said.

———

H.L. West, in his nineties now, cannot recall that mill, that idyllic realm. There were no parties, no dances in his world. At age four he had lain near death from Spanish flu, his lungs full of fluid, his fever spiking, hallucinations crawling up the wall. Spanish flu killed more people worldwide than the Great War. In Alabama, schools, stores, and businesses closed as people tied rags and handkerchiefs around their faces to avoid being infected. West's family could not afford medicine or a doctor, and children like him just died in the pines, victims of their class as much as any microbe.

In one of his first memories, he can recall choking in his bed, remember asking his father for a soda cracker. His father walked a mile to the store to get them, and when he came back, he held them out to his son, hoping he would rise from his bed, walk over to him, and take them. But the boy was too weak, and he can still see his father's hands as he broke them up and fed them to him. "The best crackers I ever ate," he said.

These were the people who came to Greenleaf's mill village for salvation.

In '33, his family moved to a company house at 115 D Street in the village. His mother, father, and seven brothers and sisters crammed into the small house, where the only source of heat was one coal stove. There was no free doctor that he can recall. His father was paid in steel tokens and earned less than his family ate, less than he owed.

"It wasn't all that good," he said, "but we didn't know any better."

He joined his father in the mill that year, when he was sixteen, sweeping scraps of cotton and lint. He routinely worked eighty hours a week, never a penny of overtime because there was no such thing as overtime. One day, when he stopped and stared at a piece of paper he had swept up, his broom going still for just seconds, his boss spotted him.

"You better git back to work," the boss yelled.

"I'm workin'," he said, and swept faster.

The boss, a big man, walked over and stood over him.

"I was just looking at this paper," H.L. said.

The boss just stood there, looking down at him.

"There's a barefooted boy outside, just like you," the boss said, "wanting your job."

You just took it then, because there was no other way to be.

Then the union men came to town.

———

It had been coming, this trouble, for a long time. World War I had brought a boon to the industry—war meant uniform contracts—and Southern cotton mills prospered even as working conditions remained hot, dirty, and dangerous. Subsistence, not prosperity, was all a worker could expect even in the best of times. In the Roaring twenties, dresses went from ankle-length to thigh-high—not here, of course, but in the wider world—and shorter skirts meant less cloth, and less yarn. Mill owners, trying to increase production, went to faster machines and spread their workers more thinly across the floor, working them half to death. A wave of strikes rippled across the South, from Elizabethton, Tennessee, to Gastonia, North Carolina. Mill owners hired thugs to put the strikes down hard. In Gastonia, the strike turned bloody in the spring of '29. The city's police chief was killed, and a strike leader, Ella May Wiggins, was murdered on her way to a rally. Soon, it became clear that the union, the United Textile Workers, could not stand against mill bosses who owned politicians, and could, with a telegram, summon strike breakers or even the National

Guard. But the noise they made had nudged Roosevelt toward his minimum wage act, and emboldened the unions.

Men with Yankee accents, bad neckties, and big ideas began to appear in the little towns, talking about a worker's rights. The hill people laughed at them at first. What good is it to wave a sign you can't read? The workers had always known it wasn't right when the mill bosses fired them for getting sick, or walking too slow across the floor, or fouling the line. But it was the boss's mill, wasn't it? They lived in his houses, drank his water, read their Bibles—the ones who could—by his electric light.

But now, these union fellows told them the president—the president, no less—said they were worth something too, worth five dollars more a week, by God. The *government* said that. And old man Greenleaf and men like him said to hell with the government, to hell with the law.

H.L. West, who is believed to be the last surviving member of what would become a textile workers union in Jacksonville, said the mill workers always resented Greenleaf. But in the summer of '33, "we hated him."

John Pruett felt that hatred first hand when he went with one of Greenleaf's sons to a city swimming pool on the edge of the mill village, one of the few places where town people and the village people came together. "I dived in, and a son of a bitch dived in on

the opposite side with a big ol' rock and hit me on top
of the head," Pruett said. "If he'd knocked me out, I
would have drowned."

The morning after the mill hands hanged Greenleaf in effigy, they did not step meekly into the weeds
when the big man's car wheeled into the mill village.
Instead, they crowded around it. His sons, expecting
trouble, had followed him to the mill as bodyguards,
and walked him through a gauntlet of men who stood
not cheering or jeering, but quietly staring, their jaws
set and their fists clenched.

There would never be common ground. The distance, across the veranda, was too great.

They had pleaded for decency, and he had flipped
a quarter at them.

———

JACKSONVILLE, Ala., Aug 2, *The Anniston
Star*—The Profile Cotton Mill here was closed
today when employees struck, protesting al-
leged failure to receive the minimum wage
provided under the textile code in the National Recovery Administration…"I'm not
going to fight," said Mr. Greenleaf. "I have offered them all I can…"

The striking men and women met in a grocery
store on the south side of the town square, to hear organizers from the United Textile Workers of America
tell them they had to hold out, do without if they had

to. The people smiled at that. You did without even
when you were at work, in Greenleaf's mill. The union
men extolled workers to chant, sing, and march, in
non-violence. "And you know, a smooth-mouthed
feller can get a lot of people to follow him," said Homer
Barnwell, whose father was a union man.

But they miscalculated, those outside agitators,
the nature of these workers. These were people who
cut and shot each other for sport on a Friday night,
people with the mountains still fresh in their hearts
and minds, people who lived by the feud. Non-violence was a new concept.

About three hundred fifty people, the majority of
the work force, walked out that summer, people with
no savings and no cushion to get them through the de-
privations to come. Their vote to strike was not just a
symbolic gesture. It meant they were willing to starve
to be treated decently and paid fairly for the first time
in their lives. They formed a picket line stronger than
barbed wire, not a barrier of waving cardboard and
slogans but a fence of flesh and blood, and it would not
be crossed. More than one hundred striking workers,
both men and women, some carrying hickory clubs,
shotguns, and rifles, surrounded a truck loaded with
yarn as it tried to leave the mill. They threw the spools
of yarn to the ground. Some workers picked up rocks
and stoned the drivers for trying to haul the yarn off
the mill property, but they stopped short of murder.
Over the days ahead, strikers boarded more trucks

and tossed yarn over the side as quickly as the few, non-striking workers could load them.

"They besieged our office, and for several hours threatened violence and injury to everyone therein," Greenleaf wrote in an affidavit that he published in a three-quarter page advertisement in *The Anniston Star*, to make sure his side of the story was told. The workers "openly declared they didn't care whether they were within their rights or not because they proposed and intended to take matters into their own hands. While this riot was still in force the sheriff of Calhoun County came upon the scene but viewed it so gingerly from his car and the outskirts of the crowd that he apparently saw nothing of interest to him or felt that it was altogether too serious a matter for him to make any attempt whatever to restore law and order."

Greenleaf did not mention that he had summoned a city policeman, and that, upon his arrival, the strikers had taken away his gun.

"Walked up behind him and hit him with a brick," Homer said. "People always wondered how that brick fell off the wall of the mill and hit him just right."

For Greenleaf, the strike was a criminal act. He grew red in his face and sputtered, even in his writings, which were so verbose and convoluted that most mill workers could not make them out.

"We hear today that a very prominent labor leader has recently addressed a church assembly here...and given such advice and counsel as has apparently caused 'the law to be laid down' to us in terms which it would seem must mean we can only quit business or begin to live under a rule that impresses us as little different than enlisting in and submitting to the gangster's weapons and mode of life," he wrote in one ad in *The Star.*

With an unlimited advertising budget, he spent thousands of dollars to defend his position against paying workers a few dollars more. He routinely fired off manifestos in half-page ads, including one that promised the people of Calhoun County that the mill would never run again. "Until we can operate with a reasonable certainty of having a HAPPY, CON-TENTED, LOYAL GROUP OF WORKERS, none of whom will be subjected to INSULT, THREAT AND IN-TIMIDATION AT ANY TIME…and until we can operate without the protection of National Guards or ANY EXTRAORDINARY POLICE PROTECTION WHAT-SOEVER—a condition which is not possible today."

The strikers, who could not afford a classified ad let alone a half-page one, retaliated the best way they knew how.

They attacked Greenleaf's automobiles.

One man sliced open the top of Greenleaf's convertible with a pocketknife, and workers routinely stole the valve stems from his Packard's tires, leaving the big car on four flats in the mill lot. Greenleaf began carrying a tire pump and extra valve stems to work with him and had his few loyal workers pump up his tires so he could go home. Striking workers also unscrewed the valve stems from the tires of the loyal managers and office workers, then sold them back for a quarter. Greenleaf castigated the strikers as petty criminals and low vandals, incapable of any meaningful negotiations beyond such childishness. Soon after, hearing a loud crash in the parking lot, Greenleaf raced out the door of the ground-level office. His Packard was upside down.

He had the power to evict the workers from their company houses, but that would have dangerous in such a violent time, and cost him his most skilled people.

Finally, he just closed down the mill, locked its doors, and went home to the bunker of his antebellum house, which police patrolled night and day.

———

The better-off people in the foothills sided with Greenleaf. They were frightened by it all, and considered such a rebellion a socialist uprising. Newspapers editorialized against it. Without a paycheck, and with the mill commissary refusing to extend credit, workers and their families went hungry.

Nearly two hundred families, people who considered "relief" shameful, applied to the county welfare committee for help, and 175 sacks of Red Cross flour—more than two tons—were passed out in the village. As summer cooled into fall, as the flour barrels showed bottom, the first cracks in solidarity showed.

Men and women who supported the strike grew angry as the outside organizers told them to hold fast, even as the strikers' children did without bread and milk and medicine.

One night, as an out-of-town union-organizer tried again to whip up enthusiasm, a union man named Jack Taylor had all he could stand. Taylor, whose father held one of the best blue-collar jobs at the mill as a master mechanic and electrician, came up out his seat, his face red and his fists bunched up. He waded through the crowd toward the union organizer, to fight him right there for being so full of wind as the people suffered. Paul Stewart, a staunch union man, stepped between them.

Taylor threw the first punch, which landed against Stewart's head. They traded punches and staggered across the floor, then locked arms, teeth bared, face to face. "They fought and tumbled right down the stairs all the way to the bottom," said H.L. West. "They was going after one another pretty rough."

Union men finally broke it up, but something was lost that night, something they would never get back. For the first time since the hill people filed in from the pines to take their places at their machines, their kinship, their oneness, was fractured.

The strike became civil war.

"Brothers fought against brothers, families against families, with axe handles," said Homer Barnwell. Fights broke out in yards, streets, at the ballpark, in churchyards. Women would grab each other's hair and yank as hard as they could, and children fought in the playgrounds. But what happened in daylight was nothing compared to what happened after dark.

As the strike disintegrated, as more people quit the union and said they were willing to cross the picket line, men gathered in the street, fueled by moonshine and growing desperation, and fought. Gunshots sounded throughout the night. "Momma would herd us in the corner and kneel down and hover over us, like a chicken with her biddies," Homer said. He would lie in his bed and listen to the pounding feet outside. Men were wounded, and laid across kitchen tables.

But if you ask the oldest men and women which families were which, and who was on what side, they sit mum. "There's things ain't been mended yet," Homer said.

As mill village families did without, Greenleaf let uncashed dividend checks pile up because he did not need them and because he did not want to pay taxes on them. Sam Stewart Sr. said Greenleaf hated paying federal income taxes so much he never cashed dozens of dividend checks he received. There were stacks of them in a roll-top desk. He apparently believed it possible that income taxes would either go down or go away in the future.

By winter of '33, the workers had all they could stand, and went back to work.

The next year, in '34, thousands of workers around the South would walk out in The Great Textile Strike, a failed and bloody crusade put down with gunfire and troops. Thousands of striking textile workers were herded into barbed-wire concentration camps, and others were shot to death by hired killers. But in Jacksonville there was no stomach for such misery any more, and the machines hummed on.

There would never be another union here.

Greenleaf had defied not just his workers but a president and the federal law, and he had won.

But he had seen his world order shaken.

"He believed unions and labor were taking over everything," Gardner said.

People no longer knew their place.

————

Only five months after the strike ended, in April 1934, Greenleaf resigned. He had survived the strike, but the accumulated, largely ignored debt the mill owed to the Henry family and more long-running legal feuds combined to force his exit. "The Henry family thought they could run the cotton mill better than he could," Gardner said. Greenleaf quit with more money than he could spend, with land, with everything except a mill. It should have been a splendid exile, but the old man seemed lost without his kingdom. Greenleaf spent much of his time sitting in front of the radio, downing bourbon.

The mill had, in its beginning, supplied water to

the city of Jacksonville. When the town began to con-
struct its own water system, city leaders approached
Greenleaf about buying a network of water pipes still
under his control. "They offered him fifty thousand
dollars for his rusty pipes, and he turned them down
and got mad at all the city fathers," Pruett said.

"Cooperation? Cooperation?" Greenleaf fumed.
"I know what they mean. They want me to cool while
they operate."

His retirement was bitter and wretched. The house,
instead of a great showplace, became a gothic cathe-
dral. It was crammed with furniture, magazines, old
newspapers, and trunks stacked to the ceiling.

"You should have seen the junk," John Pruett said.

Gardner had a black snake that got loose in the
house's pool room, hiding in the wall, Pruett said.
"Next time that snake appeared it was as big as a damn
boa constrictor."

There were so many cats and dogs in the house
that they could not keep them off the dining room
table, even during meals. So, Greenleaf installed a
small, crude electric fence around the table. It sounds
like folklore, but Pruett and others here say it is true.

After the war ended, another Greenleaf son, Ivan,
was killed in a car crash. An Army pilot, he had been at
a local officers' club with a friend and left in a Packard.
"Ran off the road down at Bonny Brook and killed both
of 'em," Pruett said. "He was one of my best friends."
Pruett remembers sitting down with the old man after

the car wreck, the two men drinking hard and steady.

Finally, Greenleaf spoke: "Why couldn't that have been one of Ross Pruett's boys that got killed?"

Ross Pruett was John Pruett's father.

———

The house continued to rot. The roof was full of holes. Greenleaf put buckets throughout the attic.

"You'd be sleeping, and a bit of plaster would fall on you," Pruett said. "Mrs. Greenleaf stayed on his ass all the time about fixing that roof. Early one morning I was leaving to go on home, and she was coming in the back door, rubbing her eyes. I could tell she had just woke up. I said to her, 'Where in the world have you been?' And she said: 'I slept in the car last night. I never dreamed that Daddy Greenleaf would ever sleep in a house like this.'"

Greenleaf finally put up scaffolding around his house, for repairs. "Damn if the scaffold didn't rot down before he got any work done," Pruett said.

He forgot to pay taxes now, and failed to collect rent from his tenants. "If he kept up with his business, he would have been a damn billionaire with all the stuff he wasted," Pruett said.

In 1954, he went by to visit the seventy-nine-year-old Greenleaf, who was in the last stages of mouth and throat cancer. Pruett poured them both a shot of bourbon. When he returned several days later to visit, the glass was still there, still full.

Some nights Pruett could still lure the old man

out on the porch, to drink and remember. One of those nights, on a second-story porch near the Grecian columns, the two men sat listening to the dark. "You sure can hear the mill tonight," Pruett said.

"Yeah," Greenleaf replied, "but it's not running right."

Finally Greenleaf refused to leave his living room. "He got so depressed," Pruett said. "'Best Dressed Man in Alabama' they said. And when he died, he was the worst dressed man. He wore his smoking jacket. Had ashes all over it. Let his beard and hair grow. His beard was full of nicotine."

Greenleaf died three days after Christmas 1954. Although he once owned much of the property that made up this town, he never considered it home, and his marker lists only that he was born in Littleton, N.H.

As Gardner lay dying, many years later, he summoned up the strength to defend his father one more time. It was the world that was out of whack, not his father. "We don't live in a free country anymore. You may think we live in a free country, but we don't. We live under a socialist welfare police state. We're a member of 176 communist countries in the United Nations. I was born in freedom, and I watched that taken away. The Democratic Party has destroyed my country. We didn't have enough patriots to offset what was happening so we've got the mess we're in now."

His father, he whispers, was a patriot, and a good man.

———

H.L. West went back to work in '33, when the union failed. He met his future wife, Pauline Wilkerson, there, and they would linger in a stairwell to talk, stealing a little time from Greenleaf's pocket. Eventually, he quit and went to Anniston Army Depot, earning double his salary. He never returned to the mill. In retirement, he spent seventeen years taking care of his wife, after an aneurysm and stroke crippled her. He is in his nineties now, a widower, and even with so much life and so much love and tragedy behind him he still drifts back to the mill in his mind, like the things that happened there only just occurred.

He remembers a day, after the strike, when a boss dressed him down. "I was laying up rope on frames," he said, referring to the fat coil of yarn that would be spun into finer yarn in the machines. "There was different kinds of rope, and it had to be on certain frames. This boss man accused me of mixing it up and putting it on the wrong frame. He was just a mean ol' man."

Sick of being talked down to, he talked back.

"You sound just like Hitler," he told the boss.

"You're fired," the boss said.

"I don't care," H.L. said.

He did, though. He needed that job. But before West was off the floor, the boss relented. "He knew he couldn't fire me, AND get work out of me."

After Greenleaf's death, a terrible thunderstorm tore through the town. Frances Greenleaf stood listening as thunder shook the old mansion, sending plaster raining down.

"That's Daddy Greenleaf coming through," she said. "He doesn't like the way we're running things."

———

John Pruett left Jacksonville in '52 and lived a fine life, flying his plane in an age when flight still took a man's breath away. He took farm boys and pretty girls for rides, and one family paid him with a goat. He flew and flew, all the way to NASA, and even helped bring Apollo 13 home. He retired in 1988, two years after watching the Challenger Space Shuttle explode above his head, and came home to live out his days. He died in late summer of 2008 and was buried not far from Greenleaf.

The mansion was torn down. A pharmacy sits on the lot now, facing Highway 21. Most of the people who knew Greenleaf, who knew his times, are gone. Only the very old even remember there used to be a castle here, or that a great and terrible lord once walked its parapets, watchful of an assault on the gates of his class.

homer's odyssey

He lay in the freezing mud, Germans thick as black-birds in the distant hedgerows, thousand-pound bombs falling, falling into the earth. Around him the forests splintered, towns burned, and the dead lay un-collected in the snow. Overhead, above the smoke, B-29s blacked out the moon, and artillery shells the size of garbage cans screamed across the sky. But he slept, a good soldier, hungry, dirty, too exhausted to be very much afraid, and dreamed of a blizzard of cotton, of a single, massive smokestack, of blood kin battling with tire irons and two-by-fours in the strike of '33. Homer Barnwell might have dreamed something better, something gentler, but how do you dream of skyscrapers and swaying palms when a mill village is all you have ever known?

He could see himself there, bare feet black as tar from walking on streets of smut, peanut butter on his mouth, graham crackers in his fist. He could see his neighbors, five hundred of them, see flour-sack shirts and snuff cans and severe, ankle-length dresses, their rundown brogans and scuffed, high-top shoes shuf-fling toward the gate. He could see Stewart Reynolds' pinned-up sleeve, see Pop Romine's scandalous, un-done overalls. He could see children among them, eleven years old, even younger, see fourteen-year-old

Clay Hammett take up a homemade bat to smack one last raggedy baseball into the dawn, then grab a brown-paper lunch sack and fall in line.

But mostly he could see his kin, see his white-faced daddy, John, lungs ruined by the clouds of mustard gas that wafted across a WWI wasteland of dead horses and twisted wire, coughing up his life on the stoop of their company house. He could see his momma, Bertha, the angel, her limp hand in his as she led him two miles in baking heat to a swimming hole, when all she wanted after her shift was a quiet moment and a cool trickle of breeze. In the good dreams, the best ones, he could see his brothers and sisters, William, Evelyn, Carrie, Carl, Lola May, and Ethel, squirming through an endless sermon in the Pentecostal church, knowing that there was a whole wash tub full of banana puddin' waiting for them at home. "I could see 'em," said Homer, an old man now. "I could see 'em plain."

He dreamed it and daydreamed it. Homesickness settled hard in that death and mud.

His sister, Lola Mae, wrote him letters, but it was his Momma's voice in his head when he opened them, because he knew it was her thoughts. "Momma'd never been to school a day in her life, so Lola Mae wrote 'em for her…I guess they wrote me ever' day." It was the story of the village they wrote him, who was sick, who died, who had gone to war, who had been hurt in the machines. He read them a thousand times, folded and re-folded them until the creases, black edged from the battlefield grime on his hands, finally cut the paper in two.

"I never had been nowhere. Well, I might've been to Birmingham. All my life, that smokestack at the mill was our landmark. As long as I could see it, I knew I wasn't lost. It was hard to see, from over yonder."

———

He can no longer hear well, his eardrums pounded by the big guns he manned to fight the German with the Big Red One, and his eyes, still bright behind his bifocals, are weaker now. But his memories are sharp and glittering, like pieces from a broken mirror. He was born on October 23, 1924, his mother and father among the first of the mountain people to seek salvation in a cotton mill, discover its disappointments, and yet remain, because there was nowhere else to go and nothing to reclaim. He ran its streets as a boy and walks them now in a deliberate, careful stride, and the ghosts in every house still speak to him, softly, as he passes by.

"We could've all run away," said Homer.

Then he smiles.

"I guess," he said, "we'd a just wound up in another mill."

The draft took some of the best of them, across generations, and people flew flags from the little houses and put cardboard stars in their windows, if they had a boy at war. They buried them under those flags, war after war, but even if you came home whole,

to this place, the machines and lint would finish the
job the war began. The trick, here, was to survive the
bullets, bayonets, and bombs, then survive the homecoming, and endure the peace.

———

His daddy soaked up five bullets before he ever went
to his war.

Now that's a man for you, the people here always
said.

Homer's father grew up in the Georgia mountains, and went to work in the mill in '15 or '16, before the outbreak of World War I, before he married
Bertha. On a weekend night in '17, a night when the
whole village seem splashed with moonshine, he got
into an argument with a Jacksonville policeman, shot
him, and was wounded five times himself.

"It was a case of mistaken identity," is all Homer
will say.

John Barnwell recovered just in time for the draft
in '18. He fought his way across the Argonne Forest
with the rest of the 42nd, the vaunted Rainbow Division, the mustard gas leaching into his lungs. But
even though the German machine guns cut the trees
to stumps and killed every living thing around him,
he was never shot again. He took his war wound home
with him deep inside his chest, to work the same job
in the same smothering mill.

"They put an ad in the paper that said, 'Good working conditions,' but you know how that is," said Homer.

The first generation worked a ten-hour shift, Monday through Friday, and a half a day on Saturday, for about a nickel an hour, about $2.50 for the fifty-five-hour week. They were paid twice a month, always on the weekend. Children worked for a fraction, as little as a fifth of a grownup's pay.

"Didn't nobody get nothin' ahead," Homer said, of all of them. "I can still see their faces, see the hurt in them. Them people suffered, boy. But all people could think of was gettin' on."

They are all gone, that first generation, used-up shells buried in the red clay, lungs full of lint.

If that were all there was to it, this village, it would only be a story of misery and nothing more.

"Gosh," Homer said, "it was their life."

On Sunday, his mother cooked feasts from beans, cornbread, and potato salad, cheap, filling, delicious, and made banana puddin' in a wash tub.

"I ate till I made myself sick," Homer said.

She made tall stacks of graham crackers and peanut butter, and that was better because it was travelin' food. Homer hated to stay still for long, then, because he might miss something. Like all the children here, he roamed through the yards and houses, welcome at every door.

"I had 136 mommas and daddies," he said.

One day a week, just one, Homer was a prisoner in the house, forbidden to roam the village and hear its stories and greet its people, and could only stare out the window, and watch the mill workers file by.

"Momma washed my underwear that day," he said. There was only the one pair, what people here called their long-handles. "And I had to stay in the house till they dried."

No one was better than anyone else in that grid of small houses, because everyone was the same.

"I used to tell people I lived on May Pops and artichokes till I was in third grade," Homer said. "Daddy would give me a nickel to go to bed without supper, during the night he'd come in an' steal it, then charge me a nickel and whip me for losing it."

You smiled at poverty, the way you whistled walking past a graveyard.

"I always walked in the shade," he said.

His Momma, Bertha, had a Sunday dress, and two dresses she worked in. "There wasn't no clothes closets in them houses," Homer said. What would they have used them for?

It is the only time his smile slips, and he almost cries.

"But there was so much love in that place, a transfer truck couldn't haul it out," he said.

He cannot remember exactly when he first realized the cost. He does remember a day, just another day, his father had sunk down on the porch, exhausted after walking home from his shift. Something made Homer look up the street, then down the street, and there he saw the same scene on porch after porch, as women and men made it only as far as that and melted onto the stoops. It was as if some painter had captured the same scene on canvas a dozen times and hung them in a long, bleak hall.

His father's health worsened in the lint, heat, and damp.

He never complained, just accepted it as his fate, his place.

"Daddy wasn't a talker," said Homer. He was so quiet that, to this day, Homer has trouble remembering things he said. But he never knew his father when he did not cough.

"I saw him so tired he couldn't get up the steps," said Homer. "He'd just sink down there on that first step," and try to breathe.

There were mornings when he was, at first, unable to get out of bed, but there was never a morning he did not get up. A man who was too sick to work was no use to the mill, and a waste of a good house.

"You couldn't lay out," Homer said. "Nobody laid out. There was too many people wanted your job."

Homer's mother never denied her children anything that was in her power to give them. There was never money, so the only precious thing left was time.

"She'd come home wore out, and we'd be settin' on the back porch, and we'd beg her to take us swimmin'," Homer said. She would get up without a word and lead them down the road.

"If there ever was an angel on this earth, it was my momma," he said.

His mother and father kept him out of the mill when he was a child. But when he was sixteen, he took a job carrying lunches into the mill. There was no lunch hour, not even a break to clean the webs of cotton from their faces, so they would eat at their machines, picking cotton out of their food. "They used a whisk broom to try and brush each other off," said Homer, who delivered sandwiches and drinks from machine to machine.

"Mr. Woodall, at 8 A Street, always ordered an R.C.," he said. "Ethel McCurry at 69 C Street, a hamburger. I can see 'em right now.

In '41, as the Japanese bombed Pearl Harbor, his father lay dying.

He was finally ready to talk. He called his sons to his side to tell them what to expect. Of course, they would be drafted, they would go to war. "He didn't talk much, you know, but he tried to tell me some about what to expect." John Barnwell died on December 20th.

After his death, Homer's brother, William, helped his mother make their living in the mill, till he was drafted a few months later. He was shipped off to the South Pacific on a destroyer. Homer then took his place beside his mother in the mill.

As his eighteenth birthday neared, he waited for his draft notice, waited with a certain amount of dread that it would come, and a certain amount of shame that it didn't come.

He got his letter in winter of '43.

His Momma sat on the floor, clutched her arms around her knees, and wailed.

"If I was scared, it was for our family," Homer later wrote. It was one thing to be put in harm's way. It was another to go to war knowing that he was leaving his Momma in hardship. If she were hurt, there would be no house to come home to. It would be given to another family overnight. "It seemed to me we were leaving all the womenfolk stranded," Homer wrote, "but the same thing was happening to all the families around us."

Empty caskets were carried through the streets. Headstones were erected over undisturbed ground. Louis H. Harris, of 111 D Street, was taken prisoner after the fall of Corregidor, and starved to death in a Japanese prison camp. James E. Johnston, of 36 A Street, was killed on his ship. Olin L. McCurry, of 69 C Street, and Renay W. Webb, of 98 D. Street, died in combat. George Robinson Jr., of 73 C Street, was killed when his ammunition ship blew up off Marcos Island.

———

Photographs taken by his buddies show a good-looking boy who looks more fourteen than nineteen. His helmet looks too big for his head, which makes his head look too big for his body.

He did thirteen weeks of basic training at Fort Bragg and was homesick every night. "But the chow was good," he said. "We had pork chops, mashed potatoes, gravy…"

He was assigned to the 3rd Army, 1st Division, 16th Infantry, and after basic training he boarded the U.S.S. Santa Barbara in Camp Kilmer, N.J., on Nov. 19, 1943. "I still didn't know where we was goin'." He was not seasick. "But a lot of 'em was."

It was the first ocean he had ever seen.

The ship joined a convoy, the safest way to cross the Atlantic then, and zig-zagged across the ocean, to make it harder for the wolf packs of German U-boats that preyed on the allied shipping. They crept into South Hampton in thick, cold fog on Dec. 1st. He was still homesick, but it was easier. The city was blacked out, "but we found the beer joints by the smell," he said.

He saw the destruction caused by the German bombers and he thanked God that the ocean was so much wider between the Germans and home. He tried to joke with the British about their awful weather, but found they did not have a sense of humor about rain and fog.

They put him in the artillery, and after months of rumors, he boarded a transport ship to take the fight to the Germans and commence their destruction. As the first few waves of soldiers waded ashore and died in the sand and surf of Normandy, he and his friends waited and fretted beside their big guns, their transport ship rolling in the rough seas for six days. Finally, he and his buddies rolled their giant cannons onto the beaches. "There were so many planes they covered up the sky," he said.

The nightmare of the beaches blended into the nightmare of the hedgerows, which were filled with German snipers. "It seemed like the hedges were endless, row after row."

In a place called St. Lo, pinned down by the Germans, he hid in a hedgerow and watched eighteen hundred allied bombers level the enemy's gun emplacements on a target called Hill 192. He found out later that his cousin, Bokey McClellan, was in the crew of one of those bombers as it droned overhead.

His gun crew killed Germans they never even saw, with 155 Howitzers and ninety-five-pound projectiles that could travel eleven or twelve miles. He fought through Corbeil-Essonne, Meaux, Soissons and Laon, to Maubeuge on the Belgian border. "We fired on crossroads, towns, rolling barrages in front of the troops...what they called 'softening up the area.' You'd fire all night long. That works on a soldier." Along the way, he broke his foot and cracked bones in his legs when a seven-ton cannon sagged in the soft mud and a piece of it pinned him to the ground. If the ground had been firm, or frozen, it would have cut him in two. After a few weeks in a field hospital, he was back in combat.

The trek across Belgium, through Mons, Charleroi, and Namur, stalled in the Hurtgen Forest. He huddled there, cold and wet and miserable, and wished he were back home even as he knew he would rather die than show his face there in the middle of this war. The village was not a place that tolerated weakness, cowardice. It was not a place that accepted shirkers.

"I knew that if I was back home, all my buddies would be gone, and everyone would be saying, 'Why ain't he there?' They'd wonder why that feller's son didn't have to go and mine did. They were proud to have a big star hanging in the window."

Around him, the blasted, black trees, mostly just stumps, mocked the name of this place, the Hurtgen Forest, on the Belgian-German border. Here, the soldiers' C-rations froze hard in the can, their feet went numb, and their eyes were red from lack of sleep and the strain of watching, always watching, for the German tanks that seemed carved from a single, impenetrable hunk of steel. The men called the forest, "the Meat Grinder," where one in four who fought would die.

Here, he saw things he never dreamed of, even in a mill town, where the bloody bandages were the cost of doing business. "Our own artillery fired on us," he said. "A piece of shrapnel cut a boy's face off, and then embedded in another boy's shoulder. Companies fought all night long and then found out they were fighting each other...when the wind shifted." The German planes, coughing and sputtering on their synthetic fuel, groaned through lead skies. "Sounded like an ol' washing machine motor," Homer said.

Eisenhower had promised the troops a turkey dinner on Christmas Day of '44, but Homer ate a can of corned beef hash. "Slid out froze, like a popsicle," he said. "I went sixty-three days without a shave, or a bath."

He slogged through the Battle of the Bulge, wishing for the skies to clear so that the Allied planes could give them air support, and hoping the Germans would run out of gas for their tanks, which had once seemed invincible. The snow drifts piled up twenty feet high.

But the clouds did part, and the Allied planes bombed, and the German tanks ground to a dead stop, their fuel tanks empty. His mother had prayed the tanks dry.

He has a faded map tucked into his photo albums and memorabilia of the war. It shows the route of The Fighting 1st, shows his odyssey from the beaches of Normandy all the way into Czechoslovakia, from December 1944 to May 1945, when the war ended. They either fought or chased the Germans the whole time. He had been a good soldier. He did what he was told.

He even earned a Bronze Star, and he will not talk much about that, either.

Somehow, the Army forgot to give it to him, so he just went on home in November 1945.

The mill, he hoped, was hiring.

———

He came home without telling anyone, and walked through the streets in his uniform.

There was no parade here, although people did wave.

When he got home, he asked his brothers and sisters not to tell his Momma he was home. "When she gets off," he told them, "I'll walk her home."

But it has always been hard to keep a secret here.

Someone told her, as she hunched over her spinning frame, and she did the unthinkable.

"She walked off the line and come home," Homer said.

The technology had changed a little. Instead of brushing each other off with brooms, the workers now used compressed air to blow the strings of cotton from their face and clothes. "The poor ol' thing didn't take time to blow off," Homer said.

She came running up A Street, tendrils of cotton hanging from her like Spanish moss, weeping, hollering, praising God.

———

Homer reclaimed a place in the mill. But one day, not long after his homecoming, he just looked up from his work and knew he had to leave. After all he had seen, all he had been through, he knew he could not spend his life there in the noise and roar. He had seen too many men with pinned-up sleeves, seen too much blood. "I probably would have never left, would a spent my life there," Homer said. But the war shook something loose in him, shook it so hard it broke tradition and inertia and dependence, all at once.

The war was the end of the village as he knew it, too. The parochial nature of the mill, for good and bad, was unraveling, and people were looking beyond the village, in a post-war economy, for work. They had mobility now, were buying junk cars for one hundred dollars or less to drive to other plants, other places. Some of them were even looking all the way to Detroit, where a man could get rich, it was said, on the assembly line. The mill would spin on, employing hundreds, but the village was changing under the tires of the automobiles. Some of the hill people just went home, and drove back into town from the pines, their rusted and ragged cars forming caravans along the country roads, their headlights—and as often as not, just one working headlight—cutting through the dark. The women and men would lean against the warm hoods and talk and smoke, mixing nicotine with the lint in their lungs, until the whistle sounded.

"This place kindly come apart," Homer said. "And the people scattered. Me, I run a pool hall, seventeen years. I never did get good playing, but I sent a lot of boys home feelin' bad who said they were."

He married Reba Tillery, who worked in the mill office. Later, Homer went to work with the City of Jacksonville's Gas, Water, and Sewer Maintenance Department, till his retirement in 1986.

In June of 2004, the Army's paperwork finally caught up with him. Homer, along with another overlooked soldier named Morris Beal, was finally awarded his Bronze Star. A retired Army Colonel in a sport shirt pinned it on him at a City Council Meeting.

"On behalf of a grateful nation," the Colonel said.

His father would be proud of him for winning a big medal, he is pretty sure.

"I know my Daddy would be proud," he said, "that I didn't spend my life inside a mill."

He left the mill, but not the village, not the people. He cannot even imagine leaving it, where he knows all the ghosts by their nicknames. He lives there, still, in a refurbished company house the company has not owned in a long, long time.

He never lost sight of the mill's smokestack again.

Even after they torn it down, he could see it plain.

the guitar man

The Country Mountaineers, sharp in snap pearl buttons, hair swooped back with a handful of dime-store pomade, were playing Dwight Hall in Gadsden on a Saturday night, a sold-out triple-bill with Sonny Simms and Grandpappy Lee Bonds. The metal folding chairs were jammed wall to wall with lintheads and smoke necks, with doffers, spinners, and weavers from Profile, Marvel, and Blue Mountain, rubber workers from Goodyear, steel workers from U.S. Pipe. Their hands crashed together in three-quarter time, and floorboards trembled under steel-toed boots. They were second-generation mill and factory hands, mostly, people who grew up under smokestacks instead of pines. But tonight, the boys on stage were singing them the country they believed they could remember, singing them so close they could smell the woods on fire. There was James Couch, and Jack Andrews, and the rest of the boys. And on rhythm, picking a yellow Gibson like it was going out of style, was Charles Hardy, one of the best front-porch guitar-pickers these people ever heard. It was northeast Alabama in the 1950s, in a dry county, and the only place to get rockin' was the convention hall.

Rollin in my sweet baby's arms

Rollin' in my sweet baby's arms
Gonna lay around this shack
Till the mail train comes back
Then I'm rollin' in my sweet baby's arms

It was just wood and glue, strung with steel, but my God, he could make that thing talk. He was bad to drink then. "I needed a pint just to get goin' good." But his fingers knew where to go.

He played with a working man's hands, a cotton miller's hands, and that might be why it sounded so good, why it sounded true. A guitar was about bending steel, pure and simple. You mashed steel with flesh, hard, to make it sound sweet and clear, each string, each tone, distinct and free of the ones around it. Any damn fool could strum. He sang the same way, loud and clear, with a little squall in it, and you could hear the Johnson grass and the red dirt in every word. He sang the popular songs, radio songs, sang Ray Price's "Crazy Arms," and Hank's "May You Never be Alone Like Me," and the hopeless, soul-twisting "I Cain't Help It…"

Today I passed you on the street
And my heart fell at your feet
I can't help it if I'm still in love with you

It was all about loss, that music, but as he sang it and the Gibson grew warm in his hands, he was happy, complete.

Crazy arms that seek to hold somebody new
But my burnin' heart keeps sayin' you're not mine
My troubled mind knows soon, to another you'll be wed
And that is why I'm lonely all the time

"I could play a little bit," said Charles, who is in his seventies now. "People said I was kinda…" and he stops, as if the idea is too hard to get out. "People said I was gifted."

"That very night," he said, dreaming back, "I had my chance at the big time. I had a shot at the Opry."

In the auditorium that night was a man named Sammy Salvo, a recording artist and record producer with big connections in Nashville, and with the Grand Ole Opry. He had some hits, like "Julie Doesn't Love Me Any More," and he had glided into town on an honest-to-God tour bus. Shaking his head in admiration, he walked up to the boys after the show.

"I want y'all to play a show with me," he said. "I'm taking ya'll to Nashville. Y'all go get on the bus."

James Couch, who played lead guitar, mandolin, and some steel guitar, told the Nashville man he had responsibilities at home.

"I got to go to work tomorrow," he said, and walked off.

Charles just stood there, caught between a dream and a real life of hard work and low pay in the Jacksonville cotton mill.

"You boys ain't got no business working," Salvo said, and laughed.

He turned to Charles.

"Go get on the bus."

Charles had a wife at home, Sarah, and two children, Frankie and Vanessa.

He pictured the phone call he would make, from a truck stop or hamburger joint near the Tennessee line.

"Baby," he would have to tell her, "I'm on a bus to Nashville."

The bus idled in the parking lot.

His feet wouldn't move.

He would have done it anyway, would have risked everything, even Sarah's wrath. But the truth is, he was just scared, scared of losing another job, a real-life job, and, more than anything, scared of having a dream flung to his lap with a few seconds to grab it or let it go.

"I loved that guitar," Charles said, dreaming back a half-century, more. "That guitar was my life."

His life, but not his living.

"I reckon I won't," he told the man. "I got to go to work tomorrow too."

———

He learned it from his mother, a banjo picker. They would sit on the porch of their house near Asbury Church on the Roy Webb Road, her on banjo, him with an old guitar. The first song he ever sung was "Comin' Round the Mountain," and they would sit and play until his mother, Julie, had to go work her shift at the mill. "I was eleven years old," he said. "She could play that thing, boy. 'Going Down Cripple Creek,' all them old songs." As a boy he dreamed about the Opry, and as a young man it seemed like he might be on his way. In the late 1950s, he and James and Jack and the other boys even had their own radio show on WHMA in Anniston, an hour of live music sponsored by Jim Walter Homes.

He had never read a note of music in his life.

"I picked by ear," he said.

He could have made a good living picking in beer joints, but in a dry county there was no place to play except dances in skating rinks and high school gyms and the occasional big show at the auditoriums. He fed his family on the day shift at a succession of mills, and he was working at the Jacksonville mill, at Profile, the night he turned Nashville down.

"He always said he did it for me," Sarah said. "I don't think that's true. He went, when he wanted to go. He went out to California once and stayed gone a week. Said he went to help some guy move."

Either way, the regret sunk in like snakebite.

The Opry never came so close again.

He worked more than a decade more in the mills in the late 1950s and into the 1960s, and worked the Jacksonville mill till the bosses told him not to come back. The bosses had people waiting at the gate, begging for work.

"I was hittin' that bottle pretty hard, then," he said.

For eight years, he worked in mills in Blue Mountain and in Anniston, and picked and sang on the weekends with the band. In the mid-1960s, he got drunk and got thrown in jail. He pawned the Gibson to get himself out. The pawnbroker told everyone it was his guitar and asked more for it than it was worth.

"I didn't get to go to the shows with him, then, because I had the kids, and no baby sitter," said Sarah, who had four more children with Charles, praying he would change. "And every place he played there'd be some guy with a bottle, and he'd go with him."

Finally, after drifting from job to job, bleary eyed and befuddled from the night before, he wound up at Marvel, in nearby Piedmont. Marvel (pronounced Mar-velle) was a long-running textile mill that made comforters and bedspreads, mostly from polyester. Its machines, in the late 1960s, were notorious. Charles Hardy saw one man lose an arm, but, like the Jacksonville mill, it was a means of survival. "Jobs was hard to come by, and I was glad I had one, after everything," Charles said. "I loved that whiskey better'n a hog loves slop."

He was borrowing a guitar now, when he played. In March of '70, he and the boys played a party, and he drank a lot of white whiskey. He shuffled into work the next day, bleary eyed. "It guess it was still in me," he said.

He had sung one of his favorites the night before,
and, like the liquor, it was still in his head and on his
tongue.

Oh please, release me, let me go
Cause I don't love you any more
To live together would be a sin
Release me, and let me live again

He worked a machine called the Garnett. It was
used to process giant sheets of polyester, to tear and
flatten them into a web so it could be used as a filling
in comforters. It was taller than a man, with massive
rollers, "with teeth on it like a hand saw." He used a
long stick, like a broom handle, to work its controls.

"Nobody got too close to that thing," he said. "But
it had broke down on the second shift, and the boy
who worked before me on second had used a piece of
baling wire to tie one of the belts in place. I caught myself on a piece of that wire, and it threw my hand into
them rollers."

It started eating him alive.

An inch at a time, it pulled him into the teeth of
the machine. He was alone in the big room—there
were always supposed to be two men there but the
other one had gone to talk to the bosses—and the rollers, with their saw teeth, pulped his arm but would
not let him go. He fought it, beat it, but it just kept
grinding. The blood ran into the gears, onto the floor.

"It took it three minutes to take my arm," he said.

He finally jammed it with a broomstick.

He almost bled to death, anyway, hanging there, before someone noticed.

"It was my pickin' hand," he said, but if it had been his chording hand, it wouldn't have made any difference.

"I stayed drunk two years."

———

People would see him in town after that, working off a fine, cutting weeds one-handed with a slingblade.

"There was magic in that arm," Sarah said. "He gave up on living for a good long time. It was God's way, I believe. It was His way, to make him see where he was going."

But Charles was not speaking with God then.

He worked about five more years at Marvel.

"Then I'd come home and cry all night," he said,

He would wonder if it was all destiny, if he was cursed for turning his back that night on his dream. He screamed at Sarah about that, and blamed her.

He hated his life so much he even refused to sing, as if the same machine that took his arm had torn out his tongue.

People would ask him to sing, kin and friends, but he sat silent.

The words tasted like gravel.

Sarah went to work at Marvel, to help make their living.

———

He does not remember when it broke in him, that hopelessness, or even why. He just remembers sitting by himself in the house, years and years after he lost his arm, and these words coming out.

Her lips are warm
While yours are cold
Release me, darling
Let me go

"I sat there and cried like a baby," he said.

There are no pat and perfect stories in the mills. He did not live a perfect life, and, from time to time, slipped back inside the bottle. But he loved the music again. He saw his boy Frankie became a professional musician with his Daddy's voice and his Daddy's skill. All his children would pick or sing, and their voices ring through the Fourth of July concerts and small music halls here in the foothills. "I prayed that one of them would get my arm," he said. "I didn't know all of them would." He sang with them, and, sometimes, when he saw a man with a guitar, he would chord as the picker played.

His heart started getting bad in '87, so he quit the whiskey. He has survived prostate cancer, and surgery on his lungs. He developed circulation problems in his legs, and the doctors told him to walk, so he does, but not enough. He quit smoking, started back, and quit again. "Been quit eight weeks this time," said Sarah, who stood beside him. He got religion along the way.

He has noticed since quitting cigarettes again that his voice has improved.

He will sing for you, if you ask him. He laughs at the end of every song.

He is asked often if he regrets losing the Gibson.

"It ain't lost," he said. "This boy named Red Wilson went and got it—he married my cousin. He said, 'Charles Hardy played that thing. I'm gonna keep it.' Keeps it under his bed."

———

Carlos Slaght, his kin, hosts a concert every year or so in his carport. The people sit in lawn chairs and eat good chicken and potato salad, until the music plays.

Steel guitar wails through the pines. A young man, one of the Hardy boys, does a mean buck dance. People take turns at the microphone, singing songs that have not played on the radio in generations. "Wildwood Flower" makes one man cry, because his grandmother used to sing it when he was a boy.

Charles Hardy sits in the shade, close to the pickers, so close he can reach out and feel the strings. His children and grandchildren finally push him to the microphone, and he stands there a moment as the boys tune up, his ruined, truncated arm swinging at his side.

Then he begins to sing, and you can hear the hurt in it. It sounds nothing like new country, like that poufy, sissy, over-produced mess on the radio.

It is as different as a garter snake is from a water moccasin.

It is beautiful.

"i played with bartow hughes"

They say Clay Hammett had a rocket arm, and if you hung him a curve he would knock it into the day after tomorrow. They say he could run, too, and if the catcher had the poor judgment to block the plate, Clay would go in like the Sunset Limited, and church ladies would avert their eyes. He played for the Jacksonville mill in the late 1920s and 1930s, and he will talk about it, sometimes, till you flatter him too much. Then he will say he was only fair, son, only fair. After ninety years, memory tends to ebb and flow and eddy in deep places, and there are deeper places to sink than baseball. He loved one woman, fiercely, all his life, and he asks a friend, who is over for a visit, if he knew that his dear wife Lucille had passed. The friend says yes, that she was a lovely woman, and Clay just nods. He is asked if he would like to talk about baseball some more, and he says he doesn't mind it. He is asked if he remembers any one special game, but he says no, not that he can recall. "But once," he said, "I did get the autograph of Tyrus Raymond Cobb."

"It was 1937, in Rockmart, Georgia," he said, "and we went over, the team, to see the Cleveland Indians play the Atlanta Crackers. Cleveland beat Atlanta 3–0. Bob Feller pitched.

"One of the boys pointed at this guy in street clothes and said, 'Don't you know who that is?' And I said, 'No.' And he said, 'That's Ty Cobb. Don't you know Ty Cobb when you see him? Bet you're afraid to get his autograph.' And I said, 'Heck, naw.'

"So I walked over and said to him, 'Will you sign this?' And he said, 'I shore will.'"

Then, in a break in play, he asked Bob Feller for his autograph, and Feller ignored him, and that made him mad. Bob Feller should have known not to be impolite to a man who played a boy's game only every other weekend, who spent the days in between eating cotton in a 130-degree heat, and playing patty-cake with a machine that could take his throwing hand.

Clay, a big, raw-boned boy back then, stared right into Bob Feller's eyes, and told him he was a stuck-up so-and-so.

"I hope," he said, "you never win another game."

And Bob Feller just took it.

Clay does not have Cobb's autograph any more. "Lost it in a fire from a kerosene stove," he said. But it was a just a scrap of paper, from a man he didn't really know.

For some reason, that made him think of Bartow Hughes.

"Did you ever see Bartow Hughes play? Now, he could hit, and he could run." But Bartow Hughes was not a baseball legend in the wider world, just a mill worker like him, running 'round and 'round the bases, chased by cheers, by a sound that seemed to make everything else in that hard life all right.

"I played," he said, "with Bartow Hughes."

———

It is a cliché, usually, to call someone the last of their kind.

Clay Hammett had to live a long time to be.

There were other teams from the mill village, but none like his, a team of hometown heroes who gave a poor and exploited people a reason to thump their chests and cheer.

What he could have told, light and dark, if only he could have remembered it all. In that too-short visit with friends in '03, he sat in a straight-back chair, his body still hard and tough looking, his face still handsome, and daydreamed about the machines, his Lucille, and the sound of the crowd.

Baseball, why, that's easy compared to living.

"My Daddy and oldest brother half-way farmed and sold sweet potatoes to Fort McClellan, where the cavalry trained. When my oldest brother got drafted, there wasn't nobody to help Daddy farm. There wasn't no jobs and there wasn't no money, no place but one. In 1911, Momma and Daddy and my brothers and sisters went to work there at the mill. That was it, or else. I was born in the village, the tenth child of eleven, and the seventh son. I grew up with the constant machine racket, a roar. I could hear it from my bed, them big electric motors. We had a house, though. That's one good thing I can say. Ever' Chrismas the mill gave us all a ham. That's another good thing I can say. But we was still poor. The other boys I run 'round with already worked, my brother, Buddy Williams, Bert Bragg an' 'em—them Bragg boys, I tell you, they'd kill you over their dogs. Back then, people didn't think school, like they do now. I was in sixth grade when I quit. I told my Daddy, 'I got to go get me a job.'"

The mill was called Profile then, named for a rock face in faraway New England, William Ivan Greenleaf's way of moving a little piece of his homeland down here among these people. Greenleaf would, in time, banish what he called the shame of child labor, but a fourteen-year-old boy was, apparently, man enough to take his place at the machines.

Clay cannot really remember when his first day was, just remembers being told by a boss man to pick the compacted cotton lint from the machines. But he can still recall the way the jarring and shaking of the machines made the floor ripple, as if it were liquid beneath his toes, as he reached inside.

And that would have been all there was, just that mill whistle, that treadmill of work, if someone had not noticed him playing with his friends on the diamond, had not seen a teenage boy who routinely hit the ball so far they had to send a troop of smaller boys into the pines to fetch it. Old man Greenleaf, the mill boss, gave him a scratchy, baggy uniform with the words PROFILE stitched on the front and a scuffed-up pair of spikes and told him there might be a little something extra for him, a dollar or two, if he put some runs on the board.

He joined a team of men he already knew, some of them young men in their twenties, some graybeards who had fought in WWI and went about their baseball pretty much the same way as war. There was Bailey McClellan, Albert Slaght, Otto "Hook" Burroughs, Sam Hill, Guy "Boss" Hammett, Van Hamilton, Jud "Jutt" Harrelson, Elk Hamilton, Leonard Little, Homer Wilkerson, Jess Duke, and, towering over everyone, Bartow Hughes.

Their legends were born here, in the foothills of the Appalachians, and never traveled much farther. But the boys dreamed about being discovered, like a thirteen-year-old lint-sweeper named Shoeless Joe Jackson who made it all the way from a Greenville mill to the Chicago White Sox, and then down, down in the infamous 1919 World Series.

Old men here say Clay Hammett might have done it, his limbs and mind still young, his lungs still clean, but Clay just shakes his head when asked if his dreams were so big.

It was enough, he said, to be a part of the Profile Nine. With it, he finally found a sound strong enough, sweet enough, to drown out the roar of the machines that chased him every step of his childhood, even into his dreams.

———

Before the opening game, usually with the Blue Mountain mill, they hauled the whole team to Greenleaf's mansion to have their picture made. Greenleaf did not invite them inside, but it was something, even from the yard.

The photos show rows of rail-thin, jug-eared men in harsh Depression haircuts, unsmiling, swallowed up by their uniforms. Management—Greenleaf, and the mill superintendents—poses with them, in three-piece suits. Nine bats, knicked, splintered, and taped, fan out before them. But for men who learned to hit with sawmill slabs, they would do just fine.

They were not always the product of the mill, these men. Greenleaf was not above bringing in a ringer. But the people never respected them, never yelled for them like they did their own boys, the boys from the machines. It was more than the hero worship lavished on a small-town quarterback, a native son. In its first fifty years, the local high school had never selected a cheerleader or elected a homecoming queen from the mill village. It was not just locality at play here, but class. These boys were of their blood, and their struggle.

They played only on Blank Saturday. The hands were paid every other weekend, lining up at the office to get their pay after a half-day's work on Saturday afternoon, and the games were played on the Saturdays in between. It was, say the few old men who remember it, more than a mere baseball game. It was as intense as a revival, as violent as a coliseum, and as wild as a prison rodeo. The air smelled like a carnival from the concession stand and the tethered livestock—mules mostly, saddled and tied up to the hedges and fence rails—and if someone had just thrown in a goat-roping and a midget wrestler, it would have been complete.

On the day of big double headers, the railroad ran a special train from Piedmont to Jacksonville, and what few cars there were, in the depth of the Depression, rolled up to the field groaning under the weight of passengers. Children walking to the game through the village streets would beg to ride on the fenders and running boards, so by the time the big Chevrolets and Packards finally made it to the game they were festooned with dirty-faced little boys.

It was one of the few times that the town people and the village people mixed, a free show in a time when all the money was tight. The team played to full bleachers, which was probably only a few hundred then, but seemed like a lot more. An hour before gametime the stands began to fill with men in overalls and women in flower-print dresses, not just cotton millers but tenant farmers and day laborers, sharing rough-lumber slats with bow-tied deacons from the First Baptist Church. The surrounding trees filled with little boys, and every now and then a sinner would take a pint bottle of bootleg liquor from inside the bib of his overalls and take a slash.

Ken Fowler, whose mother was a school teacher in Jacksonville then, was one of the little town boys who ventured into the village every day there was a game.

To say he will never forget it is like saying he will never forget Christmas, or his first kiss.

"Now and then someone would try to hang a mascot, a nickname on the team, but the players always rejected it. That was considered prissy," said Fowler, who is in his middle seventies now. "If you're a real man, you don't want to be called a tiger or cardinal or cub. This was hard competition among really hard men who had lived some pretty hard lives.

"There was an aura about the games. You can't see it on film and it can't really be described or explained. You truly had to be there to understand. The world could consider them, the mill workers, whatever it wanted to. But they knew they were something when they played these games."

The Nine entered the field like conquering heroes. On game days, Hammett said, the players did not yuck it up with their buddies in the morning on the cinder streets, but waited inside their houses, so they could make an appearance.

Then, just before batting practice, they came walking along the unpaved streets, along A, B, C, and D streets, to cheers. More little boys ran beside them, dreaming, because in the world of a mill village, this was as good as it would ever be. They even asked Hammett and the others for autographs.

Some of them warmed up with a hand-rolled cigarette dangling from their lips, but it was deadly serious, out in that dirt, and if there was not a little blood mixed in it was considered a dull day. They liked to fight and they were good at it, but so were the men they played, the steelworkers, rubberworkers, soldiers and such, so brawls were bloody, ugly, but quick.

But all that was a sideshow to the great baseball. They turned double plays like the Brooklyn Dodgers, and ran the bases like Cobb. They beat Goodyear, the Army team from Fort McClellan, and every cotton mill team for one hundred miles. "We even beat the college boys," Hammett said, in a time when the pretty girls thronged the first-base line, and the air smelled of parched peanuts and barbecue, not hot metal and cotton poison.

Hook Burroughs was so named because he had a curve ball that almost changed zip codes on the way to the plate, and Jutt Harrelson would take one for the team, even a fastball off his chin, if that was what it took to win. But it was Hughes at the middle of it, a man with tree-trunk legs, forearms as big around as fence posts. He could play any position and scat around those bases quick, for a big man. He had such reach he could clear the bases even if you threw it at his shoe tops, or a foot and half outside.

Some of the boys called him Dago—the reason why is lost, because he was not Italian, at least not that they know of—but Clay Hammett never did.

"Some people did say I was pretty fair," said Hammett, "but man, I liked to watch that big rascal play."

No one seems to remember their records, just that they were always winners in the 1920s, 1930s, and even into the 1940s, when the soldiers returning from World War II would become the last generation of great textile mill ballplayers.

Clay Hammett left the mill for other work before it broke him, the reason, he believes, he lasted ninety years. But he did not move away. It is an odd condition of people whose childhoods are bound by the mill. Even in old age, they are held to it.

He does not know, for sure, that he gave all that much to the people who came to see him play, but he knows what they gave him. "They were the best people I ever knew," he said. "You could see the faith in those people," he said, but he is not speaking of religion. "You can't beat that faith, in your neighbors, in your friends."

He could feel it, maybe a little stronger, on Blank Saturdays. He used to remember it all, the scores, even the plays. But he recalled, till the end, that feeling pouring in from those crowded bleachers.

"Some people," he said, "*are* better than other people."

———

As much as he loved the game of baseball, it was hard, on a warm day in 2003, to travel far from his memories of his wife. "She passed November 25, 2002," he said, pointing to a sepia-toned photo of them taken when they were still young. "She was a wife to me, boy," he said, and then he looked around the room, his eyes fierce, as if daring someone to disagree. He is asked if he has anything else to say about baseball, but he is lost now, in a place even the cheers cannot reach, cannot brighten.

breath

Eula Salter, a little girl then, used to wonder what it was like inside the mill. It was a fortress, a great, red-bricked wall. In those days, the 1950s, a man named Joe Green would hitch his mule to a creaking wagon and give Eula and other black children a ride around town. One late afternoon, in another burning summer, he drove them down Alexandria Road, past the mill.

Eula looked up, up to the second floor, and saw them.

"People were hanging out of the windows," she said, "trying to breathe."

She would never forget those people, their mouths wide open. They would lean as far into the breeze as they could, gasping, then give up their place to the next man or woman in line.

Eula watched the people, over her shoulder, till the mule slowly pulled her out of sight.

High above, a man named Leon Spears stood choking in the heat and the swirling cotton mist, waiting his turn for a breath of air. A lifetime later, he does not recall a little black girl, or a mule wagon, or anything else on the ground below.

But he remembers that breath.

"It put bread in your mouth, that mill did," said

Spears, his mouth slack from his medicines, his oxygen bottle—necessary since the brown lung disease
stole his last few good breaths—propped against a leg
of his chair. "But it cost. You paid and you paid, for
every scrap."

The medical term is byssinosis, a disease of slow
suffocation, a disease of the mills. The people who
have it, who have it bad, breathe like their lungs are
stuffed with rags.

It is an old disease. Physicians in Europe described
a respiratory disease in textile workers as early as the
eighteenth century. In the twentieth century, byssinosis was a medical fact in other countries. It choked
workers in British cotton mills in the 1930s, and was
diagnosed from the Netherlands to Uganda. But in
the United States, especially in the South, industry executives for most of the twentieth century said it was
a phantom disease, a workers' lament based more on
hangovers and laziness than medicine.

Leon Spears' only good breaths come from a
metal cylinder now. Day by day, he sits in front of the
television, the canister on the floor next to his easy
chair, and breathes short, shallow breaths. It makes
you think of baby steps, halting, unsure.

"I had a job, I had to go to it," he says, when asked
how he wound up in this shape. Ten years before he
quit, he knew it was killing him.

Like all the others who have paid for their economic salvation with their lives, he laughs, weakly,

bitterly, over the notion that he could have quit and saved himself.

He cannot recall a choice.

"Seemed like, I don't know, like it was meant to be, that you worked there," said Leon.

He can still see himself a boy, standing in the dust of a baseball field in the mill village.

"I was seventeen, barefooted, and didn't even have a T-shirt on, and I was with a bunch of boys. I said, 'I'm gonna go get me a job.'

"'You ain't,' they said.'

"'I am,' I said."

It was like a dare.

"I went in and asked, and they told me to come in at four o'clock."

He is sixty-five now.

"I have wished so many times they'd told me they didn't need nobody that day."

His wife, Linda, was from cotton mill people, too. Her grandfather lost most of a hand inside its walls. It was the last thing her daddy wanted, to see his girl vanish into that thick air.

But she wonders, as her husband does, if they were born to this, somehow. Her father came into their house with cotton dust falling like snow, and she breathed it in even before she could walk. "My daddy, brothers, too, wound up with breathing problems. My daddy always told me, 'No matter what, no matter what happens, don't you go down there.'"

But, like Leon, she had little choice. She got married and had two little boys, and then found herself raising them by herself. "This was the best thing I could get. When my daddy died of leukemia, I went to work."

Leon and Linda met there, on the third shift.

"He was my doffer," she said, referring to the process of lifting the filled spools off the machines. "He come in one evening, a little late, and he was drunk. I said, 'What in the world? What's wrong with you? You been drinking?'"

"Yeah," he told her.

Well, she thought, at least he was honest.

"I been to a wedding," he said, as if that made it all all right.

"You look good," he told her.

He was a charmer, that Leon.

She married him, anyway.

"We had some good days," she said.

A good day, then, was a steady day, when the dust had time to settle. But she remembers how the bosses would sometimes look at their watch, mark the time, and announce that they were going to see how fast their machines could run. It was without regard, or pity. The workers called it The Stretch-Out, a back-breaking, soul-killing pace that left them weak and sick at the end of the day. "And as much as they would stretch you out, the more you would try to do," she said. "You wanted to please." And the faster their machines whirled and the louder they roared, the whiter the air, the thicker each breath. "When you sit down, now, and think about it, it doesn't really make any sense at all."

———

The lint crawling up their nose, down their throat had driven them mad. It swirled and floated, light as air, specks and hair-fine tendrils, flung off the ropes of fat cotton in the card room and whirled off the bobbins in the spinning room. It draped their eyelashes, stuck in the corners of their eyes, and found its way, like something alive, under the bandanas they tied over their mouths and noses. Over minutes, hours, it clogged their nasal passages, stuck in their throats, and was drawn into their lungs.

But there seemed so much worse, here, so much that could cripple and maim, it seemed silly to worry about lint.

Leon remembers how frightening it was, when the lights would wink out from a short or other malfunction, leaving the mill pitch black. But the machines, on a separate circuit, did not die, and they roared and bit at them, from the dark.

"You'd freeze," he said, because a stumble—or even a motion in the wrong direction—could cripple a man.

Some machines were haunted, the ones where people had been maimed.

Others were just bad luck.

But dust?

"Nawwww," said Leon. "Back then, you just didn't think it was bothering you. The cotton mill was just like smoking. Nobody thought nothin' of it."

That is how the industry battled claims that the disease was anything more than a phantom. Most mill workers, like Leon, were smokers, too.

The truth lay buried deep, deep in their lungs.

The dust was so pervasive that it collected in their pockets, in the waistbands of their pants and dresses, even, somehow, in their wallets. They picked pieces of it off their sandwiches and scooped tendrils from their coffee cups. But the bigger pieces of cotton that floated down were not a danger, really. "It was what you couldn't see that got you," said Leon, about the tiny, almost microscopic bits that were drawn into their lungs.

In its early stage, brown lung is a shortness of breath, a tightness in the chest, and a chronic cough, which is worse on Monday, when the workers first re-enter the dust, than on the weekend. Bosses dismissed it for decades as whining.

But the disease gets worse over years, until the cough is persistent through the week and worse on Monday. Finally, it results in chronic bronchitis, and emphysema. Its sufferers are prone to pneumonia, and even a cold, for those with advanced brown lung, can be fatal.

A series of lawsuits in the 1970s resulted in a

cotton dust standard—the allowable amount of dust in the air—that was upheld by the United States Supreme Court. Mills nationwide, under court order, were given until the mid 1980s to install expensive filters to help cut down on the amount of cotton dust that swirled in the air. But even as mills installed the filters and ventilators that would help workers breathe easier, their own government fought against them. On March 27, 1981, this story ran in *The New York Times:*

> *A Reagan Administration official has ordered the destruction of more than 100,000 booklets on cotton dust and is holding up distribution of films and slides on other health issues by the Occupational Safety and Health Administration on the ground that they are antibusiness, a spokesman for the agency said today...*
>
> *Thorne G. Auchter, the new administrator of the health and safety agency, ordered the withdrawal of the cotton dust booklets because he found them "offensive," according to James Foster, a spokesman for the agency.*
>
> *Mr. Auchter felt that the cover of the booklets, which showed a photograph of a worker who was obviously gravely ill and suffering, "makes a statement that is obviously favorable to one side," Mr. Foster said.*
>
> *The spokesman added that Mr. Auchter wanted the agency to be objective and not favor*

*either labor or business. The booklets, and a
poster which also showed the photograph of
the worker, who eventually died, were ordered
withdrawn from all OSHA field offices by Mr.
Auchter.*

Mill workers assumed then that their lungs just filled
up with cotton. But, in the 1980s, medical researchers
discovered that bacteria in the dust triggered an aller-
gic reaction in the respiratory system, leading to permanent lung damage from scar tissue.

———

Leon and Linda worked together about ten years
before he got sick, and then, year by year, his lungs
deteriorated.

To complain, even in the 1970s and 1980s, could
cost you your job, Leon said.

"You had to show you wanted the work," he said.
"You could be out of work, be sick, with a doctor's
excuse, and still be guilty. I never missed any time,"
until he was so sick he couldn't function.

The mill, like others around the country, grad-
ually became cleaner and safer for workers, though
the cotton dust remained a fact of life. Leon quietly
left the mill in '95, retiring with Linda to their home
on the Nesbit Lake Road, a few miles outside Jacksonville. For a long while, he was a shut-in, fighting
to breathe even with the oxygen bottles plugged into
his nose, and he would reappear only on the prettiest

days, when Linda would roll his wheelchair out onto the porch. People coming home from the mill would wave, and a few would stop, but not many. For some of them, he was their future. He died June 5, 2005.

———

The little girl in the mule wagon would get her look at what happened inside those walls. In her childhood, it was the domain of the hill people, mostly. But the mill slowly integrated its work force in the 1970s and 1980s as change came to the world outside its gates. Eula Salter had five children to raise in the 1980s, and the mill was the best chance they had. "I finally did get inside," she said, "and it was a blessing, for them, for my children."

Twenty years later, she struggles to breathe. Her lung capacity is down about 50 percent. "I used to tell my preacher, 'Pray for me, so I can get out of there.'"

She knows, finally, that the people she saw in those windows were a warning, an omen.

"But," she says, "I did get inside."

the book of odell

There wasn't a lot to eat, back then. Me and some of the boys would wait for it to get dark. Then we'd catch the frogs, and cut off their legs. You'd come back the next night and you'd see their eyes glowing, and they'd have no legs. I thought a lot about it. I didn't know it'd turn around on me.

—From a Depression-era story of the mill village, by Odell Knight

The machines that shook the ground of the mill village in World War I and into the Roaring Twenties began to sputter and stall in the Great Depression. The plant did not close but the company did not spin one more inch of yarn than it could sell, and when the orders ran out the bosses hurried across the floors with their forefingers slashing at their necks. "Kill it," they screamed over the din, and in the middle of a shift the machines wound down to that hateful silence. People who had never begged, begged for bones. Mommas scrubbed their toddlers and sent them to churches on the east side, in hopes one of the rich people would invite them to dinner. Children walked the railroad tracks searching for pieces of coal, and played hide-and-seek in the mill warehouse, tunneling through cotton bales that lay rotting, two stories high.

Odell Knight was one of them, still a little boy as the Depression settled hard onto the people of the village. It was a time of deprivation, plain and true, but it was also a time when you could survive if you could peel enough brass and copper off a rich man's car, when people with no money for a doctor took their babies to a village conjurer who would breathe the fire out of an infected wound. And, if you weren't careful, you could blow up your own grandmother with a donated potbellied stove.

Here, as Odell wrote it, is what he remembers.

———

The cotton mill my mother worked at was shut down most of the time. In my family it was me and my mother, Ethel Knight. In '32, my Uncle Charley Romine died and my Grannie Jessie Romine come to live with us. She had three sons, Donald, Elmer and Harold. There was hardly enough to eat. I remember going along Big Spring Branch with my Aunt Maxie, picking watercress and wild onions that grew along near the water.

Jay and Rube Weaver ran a grocery and meat market. Momma would send me and Donald to the store. We would go to the back of the store where they cut up the meat. We would ask Mr. Weaver did he have any bones Momma could make soup with. He always gave us a bag-full, and he made sure he gave us some with a little meat left on them. He knew what shape we and everybody else were in. He and his brother were good men.

Thanks to the Democratic Party, we got free food once a month. It wasn't much but with watercress and wild onions and fruit in the summer and the help of neighbors, we made it.

———

Mr. John B. Nisbet, a member of the Presbyterian Church, would drive through the village every Sunday morning, picking up kids to go to Sunday School. I remember the old car had running boards on each side, and the car would be full, kids standing on each running board. About once a month he would pick a few of us and take us to his home for dinner...a meal equal to a five-star restaurant, for a bunch of half-starved kids. We didn't know who would get to go on what Sunday, so we had perfect attendance.

During this time I learned the catechism, a small book of questions and answers from verses out of the Bible. I had to recite standing in front of the congregation. As I remember, I was nervous as a Momma cow with three sore tits.

When I finished, a beautiful, well-dressed lady came up and laid a one-dollar bill in my hand. I ran all the way home thinking of all the ice cream and candy and other good things I could buy. When I got home and told what had happened at church, it was equal to winning the lottery in this day and time. When Momma took the dollar bill and said we would go tomorrow and buy me a new pair of overalls, I seen the dream slip away. I learned later that the Lady who gave me the dollar was Mrs. Ide.

She and her husband came down from New York and spent the summer in Jacksonville. Her husband built Ide Cotton Mill that later became Profile.

———

We played in the old oil mill that was used to make cottonseed oil. The cotton, hundreds of bales, was stacked high. We played on top of the bales and in tunnels that ran under and through the bales. One section of the mill, one that was shut down, was still full of machinery. We made some money by selling copper, brass, and iron we took from the building. I remember two Packard automobiles that Mr. Greenleaf had left to rust inside the building. We stripped a lot of copper, aluminum, and brass to sell for scrap off them two cars.

———

The winter months were hard on us. To take a bath, we would bring a large washtub into the kitchen, set large pans of water on the stove and heat the water, then pour it into the tub. A bath was usually taken on Saturday night. The rest of the week we took what's called a whore's bath, a pan of water, soap and a wash rag.

We had an open fireplace in the bedroom. You could stay warm if you stayed within four feet of the fire. Getting something to burn in them was the problem. We burned wood and coal and pretty much everything else we could find. Things got so bad one time, me, Donald, and Elmer carried toe sacks and went along the railroad tracks and picked up coal that had fallen off the train. Some of it always fell.

———

We got lucky. Somone gave mother a two-eyed cast-iron heater. We put it in one of the bedrooms. The whole family was so excited you would have thought we had a pot of gold in there. All of us boys couldn't wait to fire that thing up, and that night we did. We got that heater so hot it was red all over. We would lay back on the bed and marvel at how warm it was. Everything worked out well until one morning Grannie got out of bed thinking the fire was out in the heater. She got some kerosene and poured it into the heater and put the lid back in place, and turned to get a match to light the coal she had put in there. And then it happened. There was an explosion. It brought all of us out of bed. Grannie was lying by the bed. She was black from her head to her feet, from soot. It blew out the bricks from the fireplace. It scared Grannie bad.

———

About forty yards behind each house was an outhouse. One outhouse served two houses, a small wooden building with a partition that separated each side. It was a nasty, dirty place, always full of flies and insects. There was always a supply of old newspapers and catalogs. It was a tradition to turn some of them over on Halloween—until we turned one over with Willis Woodall inside. That got us into hot trouble.

My friends during those years was Ray Bedwell, Fred Woodall, Peck Champion, and Grady Knighton, and more who lived in the Cotton Mill Village. If we were ever able to get some firecrackers we would wait and when we seen someone go into the outhouse we slipped around behind of it and would throw it right under the hole. We would hear the yelling and cussing as we ran away.

I think back to that time and see the Old Man coming up the back alley with the mule pulling a two-wheel cart, stopping at each toilet and shoveling out that mess, and putting it in his cart. The old mule had done this so many times over the years that when the old man got his last shovel full out, the mule would take off running, and stop exactly in the right spot at the next toilet. We kids liked to aggravate the Old Man. We would get inside the toilet and throw things in his shovel. One time we killed a large snake down on the creek. We put it in a cardboard box and started on the way home to show everyone what a large snake we killed. We seen the Old Man coming up the back alley with the mule and cart, and thought we could have some fun. We got in that toilet and the first time that shovel came under us we threw the snake in it. We heard all kind of yelling and banging on the outside. We peeped through a crack, and he was hitting that snake with the shovel. The old mule got excited and ran away, and it took the Old Man about two hours to get his mule back and clean himself up. We knew we had done something real bad, and high-tailed it for home.

Mr. Pace Bedwell, who lived in the next house across the back alley from us, was a grumpy old man that had never laughed in his life, and happened to see it all. News

traveled fast in the village, and it didn't take long for
Mama and Grannie to hear about it. When I got home,
Mama, Grannie, Maxie, they got to telling me what a
bad thing I had done, but the more they talked about
the thing I had done they got tickled and laughed and it
got louder, all through the house. So, my problems was
laughed away.

———

"A few days before Christmas me and Pop Romine went
to the woods surrounding the village and brought back
a Christmas tree. Mama brought cotton home from the
mill, and she would place it all under the tree, pinching
it into little pieces to make it look like snow. We would
all get together, some of us popping popcorn, some of us
stringing it and wrapping it around the tree. We used
lots of things to decorate such as tinfoil, ribbons, and pic-
tures cut out of catalogs. I can't remember any special
gift I received—most of the time it was a small windup
toy and a small bag of candy.

"Well, there is one thing. Calvin Davis, my Aunt
Maxie's husband, asked me what I wanted one year, and
I told him I wanted five cinnamon buns and a R.C. Cola.
On Christmas Eve Calvin told me to come out to the
back porch. He handed me a sack, and inside was everything I wanted for Christmas. I hugged him and started
trying to find a place to hide them. I can still taste them.

———

Sometimes we would go and stand outside a softball
game and wait till an old softball come flying out, and

we'd grab it and run off with it, as fast as we could run. Then we would try to find some kerosene, and we would leave that softball soaking in that kerosene. We wouldn't do it unless it was a real, real old ball, with the stuffing about knocked out. But if it was an old one, we would soak it, a whole day, and then at night we'd take it out to a dark field and we would light it. You had to be brave to light that ball. And we would take turns picking it up and throwing it from one side of the field to another. You had to snatch it quick, and some of the boys would use their shirt sleeves over their hands, but that would ruin their shirts. And we would just throw it as far as we could, and it looked like a shooting star.

———

There was no lunch break for the people in the mill. The machines didn't quit running, so the people took their lunch, and ate it at the frames. Every day, Hoyt Hammett would set his lunch on his frame. And he'd reach up there at noon, and get it. He always took the same thing, a potted meat sandwich.

But one day when he reached for that sandwich, he patted his hand on the frame and it was not there. The first day Hoyt found his sandwich missing, he wondered if a fellow worker had made some kind of mistake. The second day he found it missing, he knew it was no mistake. On the third day, Hoyt got some friends to watch for the thief.

Sure enough, they spotted him, and Hoyt plotted his revenge. This time, he would make a sandwich, but different—from his family's outhouse. Hoyt put the sandwich in its paper bag on the fly frame in the same spot where it always was, and when he looked for it, it was missing. Somebody followed the sandwich thief, and watched. They figured he would eat it fast, to keep from getting caught. He took a bite, and run for the bathroom. The next day, Hoyt brought his potted meat sandwich and set it on the same spot on the fly frame. There never was any trouble, after that.

———

When we got a minor burn on our arms or legs Mother would hold the burned place up to an open fire, hold it until we yelled or cried. That was to draw the fire out of it. People did things like that then. They used smut for medicine. When someone was cut or burned, old women would slip a finger inside a cold stove or hearth and coat the wound, and when it healed the scar would be black. To wean a baby off the breast, they would take black smut from the inside of a stove pipe and put it around the nipple. This was done to scare the baby off, and get it to start eating off the table. To cure the itch, Mama mixed sulfur and lard, and it stunk so bad no one would come near you.

But if the wound was bad, they would take us to Miss Cenie, who lived in Frogtown. She scared me to death.

The one thing we sure didn't have was money for a doctor, and when we would get sick we would go see Cenie. Some people said Cenie was a witch, but I wouldn't say that. She was real, real tall and skinny and she was sharp-faced, what people called hawk-faced. She wore long black dresses and the old high-top shoes. She might have been an Indian. When you went to her, with a fever or a burn or anything that got infected, she would talk the fire out of it.

She was religious. People said she had The Gift. She would pray over you and she would quote that part of the scripture from Ezekiel. ("And I will pour out Mine indignation upon thee, I will blow against thee in the fire of my wrath and deliver thee into the hand of brutish men and skillful to destroy." [Ezekiel, Chapter 21, Verse 31]) "Thou shalt be for fuel to the fire, thy blood shall be in the mist of the land, and thou shall be no more remembered. For I the Lord have spoken it."

She would talk in tongues. She would put her mouth down almost on a burned place, and breathe it in. I was six years old when they took me to see her. It was in the summer. We had an old stove and Mama had told me not to back up on it, but I did, and burned myself bad. It was sore and infected. They just couldn't get it healed up. So Mama walked me over to see Cenie. Just looking at her gave you a spooky feeling. I tried to back out, but Momma had me by the hand.

They took me inside and she held me by the arm and studied it. She blew on it and mumbled on it. She called the Holy Ghost. The next day, it was better. I don't know if it was her talking that did it. I don't know if it healed because of her, or else she just scared the hell fire out of it. All I know is, it worked. Cenie had power. Certain *people just had a reputation like that, that they could heal you.*

———

I was sixteen when I went to work there in the mill, for thirty-five cents an hour. The Navy took me in '43 and when I got out, in '46, I went to the machine shop instead of going to work in the mill itself. Cotton was so thick you could only see thirty or forty yards in front of you. But there was a lot of chemicals in the machine shop, and I spent a lot of years in them. Did I think I was lucky? You better believe I thought I was lucky. I thought I was safe.

———

He worked forty-six years there. In 1990, at his retirement, he was whole and healthy, and believed he had survived the brown lung and trauma that had doomed or crippled so many of his friends who worked on the floor.

But the whole time, his body had been soaking up the chemicals of the machine shop, and the poisons and asbestos he worked with lingered in his system until old age. In 1993, after suffering from pneumonia, he slipped into a three-week coma. He awoke to find himself mostly gone—both legs, an arm, even the fingers on his remaining hand.

The arm, Cenie healed. The legs that carried him across that dark field, chasing shooting stars.

He had been an avid reader and wanted to write about his life. After his tragedy, he refused to read a book or magazine. He told his wife to throw away his newspapers and ignore his magazine subscriptions. "I don't want to hear anything outside these four walls," he said. Everything he read reminded him of all the things he could not do.

But like most people who grew up in the mill village, all he needed to hammer out a place in this world was the right tool. He spent five months in a rehabilitation center in Birmingham. While he was there, doctors gave him prosthetic legs. "I seen then I was going to make it," he said.

His driver's license expired while he was in rehab. He went to reapply and take the driver's test and did not bother to tell the instructor he had no legs. "If she'd known I had no legs, she'd have been more nervous than I was. She said I passed with flying colors," said Odell. After that, he went where he wanted and used a special steering wheel attachment to make up for his missing limbs. As he passed people on the side of the road, he found himself lost not in bitterness or envy but in a simple nostalgia..

"It does no good to place blame," he once said. But he hated one thing. He had dreamed, he said, of doing that book about his childhood. But the trauma of his illness took so much time from him, so much precious time, and he reckoned it would be buried with him.

Odell died in March 2008, at eighty-two. His obituary said only that he was a loving husband, father, and grandfather, and a retired employee of Union Yarn Mills. It was far short of the volume he wanted to leave behind. But in this place, where flesh is so expendable, no story is ever cut clean away. The book he would never write is—at least some of it—written here.

———

We had fun catching the snakes that lay on the limbs and bushes along the creek. They were easy to find. We used a snare made out of copper wire and string tied to a cane pole to catch them. I remember we would catch one, two or three, find a fruit jar, put them inside a jar, build a fire and put the jar on the fire. It was a mean time.

runination day,
the sound of nothing,
and the day ralph johnson
learned to fly

"You walk into any place for twenty, thirty years, you get to believing it belongs to you," said Randall Johnson, a third-generation mill worker who never worked anywhere else.

On March 14, 2001, the bosses told Randall to help set up a stage and about two hundred chairs in the cotton warehouse for a meeting between executives and employees. The workers filed in, nervous, their faces blank, unsure. The quiet was always unnerving, anyhow, and it was silent except for the rustling of pant legs and the scudding of chairs on the floor. You never really heard the sounds of people in a mill. They moved without sound inside that roar. But with so many workers off the line, the mill's bosses had to do the unthinkable. They shut down the machines, and the people waited in all that awful silence.

They were all there that day, doffers, spinners, openers, sweepers, all of them. Some were third-generation mill-workers, and a few could trace their lineage back even deeper, to the first generation. "They'd been telling us everything was fine, so nobody, I'd say, really knew what was coming," Randall said. It could be that the company just wanted to say thank you for their hard work, or just wanted to reassure them, again.

He sat, waiting, thinking about his third day. He graduated from high school in May of '89, took ten days off, and went to work at the mill in June. The rule was that if you were late to work in your first ninety days, you were fired automatically, and the other workers laughed at him because he was so nervous about getting to work on time. On his third day, he woke an hour late. "I done blew my job," he thought, but people looked out for one another there, and someone clocked him in. His grandmother and grandfather had worked here for a few silver dimes, for meal and beans. It would have been a sin, almost, to lose that legacy in the first week.

"They put you on the worst job they had when you came through them doors to see if you could cut it," he said. "I did."

The executives came straight to the point. Due to an "overcapacity of yarn and textile production," the mill would close for good. The 197 employees would be laid off, and their machines would be relocated.

In a letter read aloud to mill employees, Jim Browning, senior vice president of manufacturing, wrote: "Effective today, we will begin an immediate phase down. Given the extreme circumstances that we are faced with, there was no alternative."

He went on to explain in his letter that, since the company's bankruptcy filing in 1999, "Fruit of the Loom has altered business strategies and realigned operations to take the company back to the core products that made it successful."

"Right then and there they told us we was shuttin' down, 'for the good of the company,'" Randall said. "They shut us down with a big smile on their face."

But it was odd how the people reacted.

No one yelled or cursed in rage.

Now that it was over, that everything was over, they didn't have any real fight in them. How do you fight against a man or woman three thousand miles away, or half a world away? How do you fight against people who are willing to work for pocket change, and draw water from a ditch?

Their ancestors had fought with guns and axe handles for basic human rights. The bitter truth was, as their jobs became safer and more sustaining, they were too expensive to keep. Now, other textile factories would restart those machines in places free of any real regulation, with much cheaper labor.

Like the grandparents and great-grandparents of the Jacksonville workers, the Latin American and Asian workers would take what they could get, because there was little else.

In the warehouse, people stared at the floor.

Some cried, but quietly.

Company officials told the newspapers it was a difficult decision to close the mill, a good facility staffed by dedicated employees, but its production was no longer required.

Sonny Parker remembers just being tired. His mind kept circling back to the same thing, the thought that was with him when he went to sleep, and when he woke in the morning:

"We did everything they asked us to do."

———

There was no big switch to throw to shut it down. The mill ran through the cotton in its warehouse. Slowly, over weeks, as one part of the production line was no longer needed, it was closed down, and then the next, and the next, and the people were laid off as their stations went silent. The mill died in pieces.

Finally, all that remained was a handful of people in the office and a few of the overhaulers, who, for a few paychecks more, began to take the place apart.

The machines, hundreds of them, were unbolted and dismantled, some sent as close as Leesburg, to one of the few cotton mills that had been spared. But others were crated up and sent to Brazil, Peru, India, China.

Sonny Parker walked through the vast rooms, hating the sound of his own footsteps.

———

A people this resourceful, who could do so many things with their hands, would survive. Some of them, like Debbie Glenn, used the layoff to break the inertia of the mill and get a better job. She went to work at the Honda plant in Lincoln, forty-five minutes away. Others were less fortunate. Some found work, but in jobs that pay only a fraction of what the mill did, with no benefits or with such expensive insurance that it consumed their paycheck. One man went to work in a factory that makes pet food from discarded food. Others are still looking for work, or have become so sick from brown lung they live on partial disability.

Sonny was one of the lucky ones. "I got a good job," he said, helping make cotton swabs at a plant in Anniston. He made twelve dollars an hour at the mill and makes $10.15 at his new job. He paid $35 a week for medical insurance at the mill, but paid $85 at his next job. After a few years, he went to work for the city of Jacksonville street department, for the security.

———

It sat empty for a year or two. The supporting pillars, bigger around than a man could reach, towered into a dark nothing. People who walked through it swore that, in the vacuum, they could hear a rustling sound, as if the ghosts of generations shuffled through the vast rooms.

The demolition began in 2006. There had been efforts to preserve it, because it was such a part of history, of life, but it was just working people's history. So the crews came, Mexicans mostly, hard-working men, to tear it down.

———

Only the lint seems permanent. The lint, at least, will linger for years in their lungs, their bodies. But you could learn to love it, once you understood the trade. "It was good to us," Sonny Parker said. But he does not expect everyone to understand.

———

"I rode by there today, expecting to see it like it used to be," said Randall, who trained as a mechanic when he left the mill. "It killed a lot of people over the years." But it broke his heart anyway to see it in pieces on the ground.

"It made me think of something my granddaddy used to say. 'The only thing that never changes, is that everything has to change.'"

———

The stories linger. Over gravy and biscuits at Hardees, the dominoes game at E.L. Green's Store, in the Food Outlet parking lot you can still hear about Pop Romine's ears, or the Sandwich Thief, or the day Ralph Johnson learned to fly.

It was in the wartime summer of '45, when Ralph was sixteen. With spring planting done, he was looking for a place to make a little money. In Jacksonville, that meant the mill. Ralph joined other boys there, all too young to draft, as a doffer, moving spools of yarn around the mill. It was like working on a stove eye that summer. "When you're that age, you don't mind it so much," he said. But he knew that first week he could not spend his life in such a loud, hot, gnashing place.

When materials needed to be moved from floor to floor, workers used an open elevator, which they signaled by pulling a chain. When the elevator was in motion, a gate came down, blocking the shaft. If the gate was not in place, it meant the elevator was either at your floor, or approaching it. It almost always worked.

One day while Ralph was in the bathroom, some of his buddies ran in and splashed him with cold water. Such foolishness was common among the teenagers. They were the only ones with the energy for it in the middle of an Alabama summer.

The next day, Ralph began to plot his revenge. He spotted the same boys slipping inside the bathroom with their cigarettes and noticed the bathroom was only a few steps from the elevator. He looked at the bathroom, at the elevator, back. Once on the elevator, heading up or down, he would be safe from any immediate revenge. Timing was crucial.

He filled a cup of cold water and sneaked to the bathroom door. "They were sitting in there, smoking their Country Gentlemen," he said.

He waited till he saw the gate swing up and open, signaling that the elevator was almost there, then ducked inside the bathroom and let the water fly. He ran as fast as he could to the elevator and flung himself across the threshold.

"That elevator," he said, "was done gone."

Instead of being just below his floor, it was just above it.

"God," he remembers thinking, "it's a long way down."

He hit almost at the feet of a woman on the line.

Her eyes got big, but she just went back to work.

He stood up to count his broken bones. He was bruised, but fine.

"Might not have been, if I hadn't been as hard as a rock back then," he said.

When he walked back upstairs, the boys looked at him in wonder. In the sixteen-year-old mind, he was a hero. How brave to dive down an elevator shaft.

But Ralph, hero or not, got tired of slaving for mill wages. "Twenty-two cents an hour, shoot, man, that wasn't nothing," he said. Ralph and the other teenagers asked the manager, Frank Deason, for a three-cent raise that would put them at a quarter an hour. Deason hotly replied, "If you ask for another raise, we're gonna fire you." They waited for the right moment, when the machines were full of yarn. "Frank come through with a hat, suit, and tie," he said. The boys approached him and asked again for their raise. He told them they were fired, and "we said, 'No, you ain't. We quit,'" Ralph said. The boys walked out, just kids tired of their diversion, as the people bound by their service to the mill, bound by their circumstances, watched them leave.

Ralph wound up working for the government, in

forestry at Fort McClellan. A few years ago, he saw the woman in the grocery, the woman he almost landed upon.

"Are you the one?" she asked.

He told her, yes'm, I am.

She walked on by.

"Like to kilt me," he said to her back.

She had no time for his foolishness, still.

The cotton millers just didn't think much of people who came and went.

———

Ralph Johnson was a well-liked man. He could tell a story or a tall tale and make you smile.

But he never claimed to be a mill hand.

You could be anyone, even a mill-shaft rocketman, and not be one of them.

You had to breathe the cotton.

You had to reach into the gears.

You had to be safe in the roar, and afraid of the quiet, to be.

sam

My brother Sam got a job with the city. The money wasn't as good, but he was free of the danger and the dust. People who loved him celebrated behind his back, and every time I see him now I think the same thing:

It didn't get you.

He still works hard with his hands, still bends his back for a paycheck. But he does it in a place where the only cotton he sees is in those fields as he drives in to work.

He is in his middle fifties, past the age when he should be running up and down mountains, but he still loads his coon dogs into the back of his pickup, drops the tailgate on dirt roads and reservations, and chases the sound of their voices up and down the lonesome dark. He wheezes a bit, now, and I wonder if it is the ghosts of the mill, reaching for him.

If you ask him if he is still a cotton miller at heart, he will tell you no, that part of his life is over. But then you open the drawer on his dresser and you see dozens of t-shirts from company fishing tournaments, company health and blood drives, company safety seminars, never worn but never to be discarded. You open a living room closet and Fruit of the Loom jackets, packed tight like baled cotton, push out toward you, every one of them like new. He went to work sick a hundred times, not for the damn jackets, but because he did not want to be thought of as a man who would lay out, not so much by the company but by the people he worked beside, his society. It was a good job—dangerous, hot, hard and nasty, but a good job—and he was glad to get it.

In my momma's farmhouse, from the basement where I sometimes write, I listen as his truck pulls up in the driveway, listen to the tailgate drop and the dogs burst out, quivering muscle and energy, hear them tear through the leaves as they surge up Bean Flat Mountain. I stroll out to say "hey" and watch. But by the time I make it out the door, most times my brother is gone, moving fast up the side of the mountain, chasing the sound. I wish, sometimes, I could hurry up that cold mountain after him and his dogs, but I never do. I am not tough like that, and I guess I never was. So I just lean against the pickup, to watch and listen. All I see is a speck of yellow from his light dancing between the black trees on a black mountainside, and then that vanishes, too.

ACKNOWLEDGEMENTS

First, I have to thank my wife Dianne and boy, Jake,
for not murdering me in my sleep as this book was
written, re-written and worried over, for years and
years. As my moods shifted like a crazy man's, as I disappeared for far too long into these stories, you put
up with me, and I am grateful, and for so much more
than that. And again, I thank my kinfolks, who are the
tap root of my writing life. Your insights and stories
are the genesis of everything I do.

I did this book, and stuck with it after it should
have died, because I believe it is important. It began
more than seven years ago, and for a slim volume has
taken up more work, more time, than anything I have
ever done.

I could never have done it alone. Many others
helped me gather the stories within, and while I know
I will fail in thanking those people, I will try.

First, I thank all the people of the mill, and the
surrounding town, who took the time to speak with
me and others, who bothered to share the stories that
make up the soul of any book. I believe you are about
the best people I have ever know, and, certainly, you
are the toughest.

The names of the village, and the modern-day
workers, hold up the paragraphs here. But one, the great

local historian Homer Barnwell, I have to thank especially, because he did everything but pat me on the head while I did this work. Homer, I kept my promise.

I thank, again, the respectable historians who have laid solid foundations of knowledge about my people, especially Wayne Flynt and Hardy Jackson. I also have to thank many others, people like Bokie McClellan, who wrote of the village and, especially, its baseball teams.

I have to thank Peter Howell, who gave me pounds of information on the mill, and tried to save it, and David B. Schneider, who complied an official history of the mill and its founders in a comprehensive application for historic status.

I thank the long-past reporters of The Anniston Star and Jacksonville News. You gave me a window into a different age, and I thank a current one, Margaret Anderson, whose kindnesses to me stretch back a lifetime.

I thank the librarians of my county, who were patient, and helpful.

And special thanks go to a small army of friends, old and new, who did some of the heavy lifting in this book. Jerry "Boo" Mitchell, perhaps the best reporter in the world at peering into the past, helped me tremendously. But there was also Greg Garrison, Lanier Norville, Lori Solomon, Megan Nichols, Jen Allen, James King, Taylor Hill, Ryan Clark, Beth Linder, and Cori Bolger.

I thank, again, my agent, Amanda Urban, for putting up with me, and my editor, Sonny Brewer, who knows his way around a sentence, himself.

I thank, again, the people at the University of Alabama, including the professors and students who heard me kicking the walls and throwing books against the door, and did not call the police, or the loony house.

But more than anyone, perhaps, I thank the readers who have followed me along on a writing life that I could not have predicted, that I am sure I do not deserve.